# THAT'S THE
# WAY IT WAS

Best Wishes
10/15/17

# THAT'S THE WAY IT WAS

## A Memoir

BENJAMIN W. NERO DMD

**To order additional copies of this book, contact:**
Xlibris
1-888-795-4274
www.Xlibris.com
Orders@Xlibris.com
739858

# CONTENTS

# DEDICATION

Dedicated to my parents.

David Manch Nero Sr.
Mary Pauline Key Nero

# FOREWORD

I remember Mr. and Mrs. Nero. I remember all the Neros. There was a story I heard, maybe apocryphal, that my grandfather, Jacob Revere once got into some racial trouble and was hidden by the Neros. At any rate it suggests that our family relationship goes back into the early 1900s. The amazing thing about the author of this autobiography and me is the difference in our childhoods. He had this strong grounding in home, family, work, and filial responsibility and I rootless, peripatetic, and fatherless. Greenwood was where I finally managed to feel safe and settled. That's where I met Ben. Why we became close friends is still a mystery. I knew the Neros all as very high profile people. Maybe fed by the story of my grandfather's relationship with Mr. Nero. The teachers he mentions as prominent in his schooling are the ones I remember fondly. Mrs. Leola Gregory Williams stands tall in my memory as one who took me to her heart. Coach Paula Thomas, who refused to fail me in math, a subject I was never good in.

Reading these memoirs has been a wonderful, thankful trip down memory lane. I have been back, living in Mississippi for over 20 years. My roots here go back many generations. My genetic heritage also crosses the racial divide through my great-great grandfather, Alfred Kerr a white Mississippian, actually married my great-great grandmother Celia. They are buried in Atala County, Mississippi, and for all its short comings, it's still my home, my comfort zone. It is where Dr. Nero and I were spawned and nurtured.

-Morgan Freeman

# PREFACE

In the center of fifty acres of fertile cotton-growing land in the early 1950s, near Greenwood, Mississippi, are a young boy and his mother. As sunset nears, their work is done, and they savor an unusual moment of respite from labor. They have taken this walk many times, and it means the world to both of them.

I am Ben Nero, and I am my mother's eighth child.

As we walk, I'm sure my mother believes she is taking care of me, but I take care of her too. I watch where she steps and listen closely to her speech. She takes this walk with all her children, but when she walks with me, it's as if no one else is around.

I take care of her because of what she means to me and because of what the land means. I know she was born of a freed slave and a white man. I know she promised my daddy, whose bloodline includes African and Choctaw ancestors, she'd marry him when he was finished with college, and I know she waited for him as she promised. I know Daddy almost went to war, but instead, he inherited this land from his freed-slave father. My parents have worked this land for most of their lives alongside my brothers, sisters, uncles, neighbors, hired laborers, and people just passing through.

My mother struggled to guide me to a life of my own, safe and free, with horizons of possibility. Despite the bigotry of the times, my mother fought for all her children full citizenship and rights for people of African ancestry. We lived in an environment of stiff-necked white people who refused to stand by the Constitution, the Emancipation Proclamation, and the Word of God. We read the Bible as a family nightly by the light of a kerosene lamp. My mother was trying to do all these things—although she never mentioned it and expected us not to mention it—in the shadow of the lynching trees groaning throughout Mississippi and the South. Mother and Daddy worked more than fifty years in these fields while raising all five of us. As their son, I know what they'd done, what they'd taught us, what they'd sacrificed.

I wanted to do something for them when I grew up.

The man speaking to you is a semi-retired orthodontist, for many years the only black one in Philadelphia and its environs—there are more now. At the University of Kentucky, where I did my graduate work, I was the first black man to be accepted and the first to graduate. At the Albert Einstein Medical Center in Philadelphia, where I did my internship and residency, it was the same: I was the first black student and first black graduate. And then, by fortune and the grace of God, I stepped into a fully functioning orthodontic practice in Center City, Philadelphia, a setting that could not have been more different from my origins.

I still work a few times a week for other practices in the South Jersey area. I love it. I love what I do. I always have. I've had thousands of patients. Through the years, dozens of them—parents of children to whom I have given advice, then the children of those children, and sometimes *their* children—have said to me, "You know, you ought to make your life story into a book." Is that what you usually tell your orthodontist? I don't know.

You see, you get to talking. Maybe it's because, and I'm only half-joking, mine is a "mouth-open business." I speak to them about what I'm seeing, about what's needed. Because body and life are one, I often speak to my patients of health issues beyond the teeth and gums. And they speak to me. Believe me, I've often been called on to give advice beyond braces, molds, and appliances. That means I have learned a lot about my patients, who often have become, through two or three generations, not just clients but also neighbors and friends. And they have learned a lot about me. That's how the business works. I'm a professional, but mine is a caring profession, and the only way I know how to do it is to care. So my patients have talked to me, I've talked to them, and from time to time, they will express pleasure, amazement, and say, "You should write a book about your life."

And I did write that book. You're reading it now. Now, I know some people will say, "An autobiography is the sign of a vain heart." Maybe so. But I sincerely hope to God that isn't true in this case. Because I understand why all those people have said the same thing to me all these years. "It's amazing you got where you are," they keep saying. "You ought to tell your story." And sometimes I wonder myself, how on earth did I make it? How did I get here? Who held me up against the wind? Who got me through? Who gave me the good words, the caresses? Who took the walks through the fields with me when I needed them?

The answer is why I wrote. My mother held me up. My daddy held me up. They taught us well. They taught us best just by being the upright, hopeful, no-nonsense, all-love people they were. What we had to do was watch them and do likewise. Which, I now know, is no easy thing. I want to tell the story of a boy who had parents like that and how those parents walked with him throughout his life. They couldn't anticipate all the problems that would come his way, and they couldn't have solved them for him. But they could and did get him ready for his tomorrows. From the moment I could understand and walk for myself, they were teaching me, "Be decent. Be good. Stand up. You will leave this place and have a better life."

This book, then, is not just my story alone. If it were, I don't think I would have written it. No, this book tells the story of being in a black community that had a vested interest in having its young people succeed. A community that did its work against the backdrop of threats to black rights and black life. My life was shaped by my parents, brothers, sisters, classmates, and teachers, all of whom worked hard to help me get on my feet. That's the story I want to tell, of being raised and educated in a caring community of people determined to help us find our own ways.

Their caring taught us to care. And now, in my later years, I see how well that network, that caring community, did its job. These children came up in Greenwood in the late 1930s, survived, got through school, some managing to avoid the murderous hatred that destroyed so many lives that never had a chance in the segregated South, and they became professors, nurses, executives, teachers, and yes, a particular orthodontist in Philadelphia, far from the farm.

So don't think of this, please, only as the story of Benjamin Nero. Think of it as a boy's life in the bosom of a family, a community, a school that lovingly and gently led him to the edge of the nest and sent him off with love. He hopes he has deserved that privileged and painstaking upbringing. He hopes, he really hopes, his life stands with the lives of his friends, family, and schoolmates.

This is the story of a family that worked hard one generation beyond slavery. It tells of two remarkable parents who taught by example and by good, old-fashioned hard work. They helped me and my siblings navigate the straits and shoals of African American life in the United States in the 1940s, 1950s, 1960s, and beyond. They knew what was happening around us, and they prepared us well. We went off and tried to do right by them, and I firmly believe and know not one of us failed in that duty. We wouldn't let ourselves.

Who else held me up so I could fly by myself someday? My brothers and sisters. We had our eye on one another. We wouldn't let anyone's grades sag. We wouldn't let anyone slough off on our chores or get into trouble in town or in school. Through encouragement, sibling competition, long sessions of homework and tutoring, and constant reminders that school was our jobs, all of us kept one another straight and true. The common phrase today is that "we had one another's backs." We did. But we also read one another's essays, looked at one another's math problems, and would have gone far to defend or rescue one another.

I have great reason to hold each of my siblings with love in my heart. Mary Jean, who was so funny, so generous, and good with children, made a life for herself in Los Angeles and, for several decades, courageously battled cancer. Colleen, a true math genius, became a state accountant, also in California.

Clyde came back to Greenwood as a teacher, principal, administrator, and town functionary. And my beloved brother David went off to succeed in the military and business.

And our network of upholding stretched to include our neighbors, several of whom were white, which was unusual at that segregated time. White children played with us, studied with us, slept over, and ate with us, and we heartily welcomed them, although we knew they could and would not offer us the same hospitality at their house. That was unheard of, and we did not test it. They were a part of our lives, though. Two of my best friends were white: Glen Buford and Nell Connerly. We observed restrictions, especially in public, for example, on the streets of our town. When together at my home, though, we were children together, and I think of them with deep fondness.

As African American children, we Nero kids were received into a loving network of other African American families and into a school of classmates, mentors, and teachers who, like our parents, instilled in us the need to achieve and excel. Self-conscious, purposeful, and vigorous, this network was not at the center of American society in the Deep South of my era. It existed at the edges, at the margins, dismissed by the dominant discourse, and it was full of people working themselves to death for their children. Our clothes were not the best. Our schools, even as hard as everyone tried, were far from the best. Our prospects were unpromising. Yet that concerned, caring community, which operated in that loving way, was working all along like a brightly lit room in a house gone dark.

And all this effort, Mrs. L. G. Williams, my English and drama teacher, brought out the best in us. Coach Leonard, who had his eye out for me and taught me about football and leadership. Our Broad Street High School principal, Mr. L. H. Threadgill, taught us to aspire to be the best despite a dark time of racial inequality and Cold War anxiety. He prepared us to be the best we could be. The great testament to this collaboration in a world that saw us as nothing and expected nothing from us, 80 percent of my graduating class went on to earn college degrees and went into the professions.

One of my greatest friends in high school was Morgan Freeman. He has earned numerous Academy Award nominations and won Best Supporting Actor for *Million Dollar Baby* and also received a Golden Globe Award and a Screen Actors Guild Award. He was already a fine actor when he got to high school, and then he followed his own winding path through the air force and onto a tough life as an aspiring actor in New York to achieve, in his fifties, worldwide recognition. For all his gifts, Morgan had to wait a long time to strike it big. We all learned persistence from watching Morgan. He began like the rest of us and developed his skills until he got it right.

As you'll find out in these pages, I hardly had a straight-arrow route to the success I've had. I wavered from Mississippi to California to Kentucky, but once I found what I wanted to do, I held on and found my way. In that, my parents walked with me, and also my siblings, teachers, friends, and classmates. And they're still holding me up, reminding me at each turn to realize the goodness I've been given.

The whole point of a book like this is to say something simple: that sacrifice works, love works, parenting, family, fellowship, and heartfelt teaching work. They don't solve all problems—I spent much of my later education catching up in areas I wasn't prepared for—but they do impart readiness and strength, and they teach the right ways to think, hope, and behave. They give a child a life to have. What a gift: a life to have. They plant deep within every child lucky enough to be nurtured in such a community indelible images of affection, purpose, and love. I can say that my life has never been without meaning, even at my hardest moments. I made plenty of errors and took a few dead ends. But those indelible images, those pointers on the road, never left me.

This first short chapter is my way of thanking people. I've named a few. Thanks is not thanks enough to my parents and brothers and sisters. I love them and miss them so much that even trying to thank them seems almost pointless. But I believe they knew what was in my heart, and much is in gratitude.

# CHAPTER 1

## GROWING UP ON THE FARM

There are so many places I can start with, so many defining points and turning points, but let me start on the Monday after my parents got married.

Mary Pauline Key married David Manch Nero on a Saturday in September of 1919 at the Nero Chapel, a little chapel built by my daddy's first cousin, the flamboyant Willis Nero, on his property near Greenwood, Mississippi. My father took my mother straight to his house on the fifty-one acres he had inherited from my grandfather, John Tyler Nero, a freed slave. That was how close my family was to slavery, and how far we've come.

On Monday, my daddy got up at dawn, as usual, making no allowance for his brand-new spouse, and made it clear she would be accompanying him into the fields that day. The cotton harvest made no allowances for anyone or anything.

Mother put on a pair of gloves and followed him out.

When my father saw that, he said, "Now, my love, you can't pick cotton wearing gloves!" Which was true, but my mother didn't know that. She worked a full day out there, though, without those gloves, in ninety-five degrees of heat, pitching in with my father and the workers. It had to be done, and it got done. She was expected to get dinner on the table too, and I expect she did and that it was delicious. My daddy couldn't cook, and Mother was one of the best cooks in the world.

Not that she was totally in love with her first full day of wedded bliss. Later, she told me, "Ben, if I had not loved your daddy so much, I would have left him the next day. That was the most gruesome thing I have ever done. The sun is hot, you are sweating, and you have to carry this cotton sack on your back. I would have been out of there."

If not for love, she would have been out of there. But she stayed. And that was pretty much the story of my parents. She and Daddy stayed together for almost fifty-four years, until my father's death in 1974. They got used to the life, and they worked very hard, seeing us children through to our adulthood, doing their best and teaching us to do ours.

I love to tell that story. It says all you need to know about both of these people who play such towering roles in my life. If I'm going to tell my story and account for how and why I achieved what I had and got to where I am against so many odds, I have to tell their story. That's because, like all children, I carry my parents with me everywhere I go, and they have made me the person I am. Not a day goes by that I don't think of them. The biggest single stroke of luck in my life, among many, was that these were the parents I got, the people I kept with me my whole life. And I can truthfully say, years after they departed this life, that they haven't let me down yet.

I can't emphasize that point enough. I have often reflected on the great stroke of luck those two were. They met, they stayed married and committed, they kept their promises, and they loved us and raised us to be strong, good people. I don't congratulate myself or pat myself on the back for it. I was fortunate. I could hardly have been more fortunate. It suggests to me that if you have that foundation, you have a good start. And a lot of people don't have that. Too often, marriages fall apart, and children are denied the stability and wisdom of parents who are always there for them.

That day-after-the-wedding story doesn't sound very romantic, but actually, it is. For one thing, it shows you how different these two people were in origins and expectations. For another, it shows how unlikely everything seemed right at the start. My mother stuck by my daddy despite a rather-unpromising start.

## Portrait of My Parents

My daddy was five-feet-eleven, stocky, of athletic build, muscular, with big, strong legs. In pictures you can see the Choctaw blood in his family: high cheekbones and a narrow nose not necessarily characteristic of an African American man. I think of him as pattern-balding. As a boy, I frequently got the job of giving him haircuts, so I knew his hairline well. He had a low, heavy speaking voice and a big laugh. He was soft-spoken and slow to anger. He loved his work. He was also active in our church, the Decell Methodist Church in Greenwood, Mississippi, as a Sunday school teacher.

My mother was five-feet-three, of average build, never skinny, and busty as a young woman. She too showed the mixture in her background. Her father's white European heritage was expressed in a very light complexion, long, wavy hair, and slender lips, with her African American side expressed in a broad nose. She had a nice singing voice and was a very good piano player. Her father had gotten her piano lessons when she was little, and she loved to play Chopin on a piano we had at the house on the farm, a piano we sold to help brother Clyde when he went to college.

Daddy was our example, and Mother was our inspiration. He was a meticulous, conservative man morally and fiscally who walked a straight line and expected no less from those he loved. His conservatism with money meant he didn't do as much to improve the house or the farm as he might have; on the other hand, he alone of his brothers and cousins came to own his farm and property free and clear. *Fair* and *thorough* are other adjectives that fit him. Both he and mother were educated people who stressed to us all that, in Daddy's words, education was "the key to the better things in life." He wanted his three boys to go into the professions, to be doctors or lawyers. He just about got his wish. His daughters became skilled professionals. Colleen used her math and accounting skills working for the state of California. David, the eldest son, would attend law school briefly and then enjoy a good career in the business world. Clyde would become an educator and return to Greenwood as a school principal and administrator. I became an orthodontist, for quite a while the only black orthodontist in Philadelphia.

Mother was the glue that held the family together. She was Daddy's partner on the farm and in raising us. She was the cook and keeper of the house and a source of comfort, love, and support for all of us.

Each had taken a very different road to get to the point at which they actually met.

If you look back from 1919, you can see that each of the great events of US history of the previous sixty years—the Civil War, Emancipation, Reconstruction, and World War I—played an important role in making my parents what they were.

Our family has a long, proud lineage in Mississippi, and there are frequent reunions among the Nero and the Moore branches. There are lots of Neros and lots of Moores still in the state. Slavery and liberation helped cement the families. Many of us lived in a single place for a long time—one house or farm or town—establishing a closeness and togetherness many of us have known throughout our lives. We shared a strong religious faith, something that has existed among the Neros since the beginning. Growing up, we had the benefit of a lot of cousins and aunts and uncles. Those are things I've found to be common among the African American families I've known who grew up as I grew up, spanning the early and mid-twentieth century, inheriting the labor of the first two free generations of blacks in this country. We were raised to help one another and know the value of family.

What we know of the family began in 1812. A slave named Nero married another slave, named Luvenia. The family was owned by Mr. Boardhammer, of Nashville, Tennessee. In 1838, a Delta plantation owner named Jack Moore bought them from Mr. Boardhammer.

Nero and Luvenia, as was usual, now took their owner's last name, Moore. They would have six children: Polk, Willis, Harrison, John Tyler, Harriet, and George. After Emancipation in 1863, the now-elderly Nero shed the Moore name and became Nero Nero. In his honor, his children also took the Nero last name—except for Polk, who, for reasons unknown, kept Moore, as have his descendants. That's why we are the Nero-Moore family.

As I mentioned, John Tyler Nero, my father's father, was born a slave and became free in his teens. He and his family were very dark and part Choctaw. Beginning in the late 1860s, once freed and on their own, my paternal grandfather and his five brothers showed a talent for business. They were both money wise and willing to invest in the future. In the last decades of the nineteenth century, they showed that wisdom in saving as much as they could early in their business dealings, and they showed investment savvy and willingness to work very hard as, parcel by parcel, they bought and cleared waste acres and timberland and turned them into farmlands.

Reconstruction was especially turbulent in Mississippi, center of the cotton industry and one of the first states to secede from and last to rejoin the Union. The Civil War and Emancipation had destroyed the old system of slave labor that had made the South wealthy, and white outrage ran deep. Whites resisted the changes imposed by Washington, and for the first decade or so, they tried to manipulate law and labor practices so African Americans had, in effect, neither rights nor property. For example, many landowners resolutely refused to sell land to now-freed blacks. Such resistance helped bring on a period of economic chaos that ruined both white planters and black laborers. Faced with the devastation, people had to compromise. This brought about the sharecropping system in Mississippi.

Blacks could work for sustenance and profit and, sometimes, expect fairer labor conditions. They were now able to bargain and compete for labor contracts with whites. If they could save enough money, blacks could ultimately own land. The system known as sharecropping was far from perfect, and in many hearts, it left legacies of resentment and shame, but it loosened up opportunities somewhat for those who were industrious and farsighted.

My grandfather and his siblings were the first generation of free Neros. The land they bought over the years was far from prime. A lot of it was bottomland or forest. You could get such land for pennies on the dollar, and while white men wouldn't sell good land to black men, they were happy to sell them the worst acres, lots with thick woods and marshes. But the Nero brothers, pooling their resources and manpower, drained the soggy bottoms and felled the trees, in time converting these unpromising parcels into farmland, on which they could grow crops, especially the main product of the region, cotton. Before they were done, they had amassed an estate of nearly four hundred acres, converting much of it into prime agricultural real estate near Greenwood.

The original band of brothers and their children had varying economic fates. My daddy's cousin, Willis Nero, would have the highest highs and lowest lows. Cousin Willis acquired the most property and had success with Blue Lake, a cotton farm and also a community, on which he eventually built a chapel, the Nero Chapel, in which my parents would be married. Also in Blue Lake were a gristmill, a school, and homes for tenant farmers and families. Cousin Willis got to be quite wealthy. He erected a large mansion-style house on the farm. That house had to be big, because Cousin Willis had thirty children by two wives. He had seventeen of them by his first wife and thirteen by his second. I have a photograph of Cousin Willis, from around 1900, posing in front of his house, with more than a dozen children, their names labeled so no one would forget. Cousin Willis showed an air of happy self-satisfaction; at that moment of the photograph, he was truly a self-made man who had triumphed over enslaved beginnings, and he seemed to know it. But there was a limit to his success. A flamboyant man, Cousin Willis adopted, unwisely, the ways of the high and mighty, affecting fancy clothes and a carriage. But he neglected to prepare for hard times, and when economic downturn hit Mississippi in the 1920s, he lost almost everything.

John Tyler Nero never got wealthy, but he earned a living working his farm. My father was born on August 7, 1887. My grandparents insisted that their children get good educations. That was becoming more possible for black children as a number of high schools, colleges, grants, and scholarship foundations were arising throughout the South to support secondary and higher education for blacks. These efforts and the people who contributed to them deserve more appreciation than they get today.

My grandfather insisted that my father attend a preparatory high school and then go to college. Many people of Grandfather's generation pushed their children like this to achieve in school since they themselves had been denied an education. That legacy was reflected in turn in my parents, who pushed us to work hard in school, persevere, finish what we started, and show ambition in our plans for ourselves. We could better our lot, generation by generation, but only if we worked very hard and maintained steadiness of purpose. There was a dual consciousness at work here: we were bettering ourselves individually, and we were also helping advance our people. Generations of African American children throughout the twentieth century have been raised on these principles. Such parenting is surely part of why we have achieved so much in such a short time.

About 117 miles from Greenwood lay the city of Meridian, Mississippi. Meridian had Meridian Academy, an all-boys prep school, where Daddy went, and an all-girls prep school not too far, where my mother attended. I sometimes say I come from "achieving people." I hope it doesn't sound too proud or conceited. I say it because I find it remarkable that my father was the son of a freed slave yet he and another brother got a chance to go to prep school. He went to boarding school by train, around 120 miles from where he lived, a long way in those days. His father was a farmer, but it was crucial to him to give his sons a chance at education. That's what I mean by *achieving people*.

Meridian was where my parents would meet. But now let's step back and see how my mother came to be at that all-girls school. Her path was quite different from my father's, but it indicated just as clearly all the obstacles and heartache that faced African Americans trying to make their way in the late nineteenth and early twentieth centuries.

## Mary Key Nero

My grandparents on my mother's side were as different as could be from those on my father's side. My mother's father was a prominent white physician in Fayette, Mississippi, and her mother, Leathie Davis, was that physician's black maid. It's a common-enough tale. As his maid, my grandmother had to look after the doctor's children. It was not uncommon for the black maid of a white family to cook, clean, and be a proxy mother, seeing more of the children than their actual mother did. As I heard the story, when the physician's wife died, he began a relationship with my grandmother, who stayed on to care for his children. In the meantime, she bore two more children by him, both of whom were added to her responsibilities. Mary, my mother, was born in 1898, of very fair complexion. A couple of years later, her brother, Floyd, was born. Floyd would live on our land later and farm part of it for himself. At some point, Leathie Davis married a man named Key, and so her last name, and that of her children, became Key.

Later on, depending on who was telling it, the story of my mother's origins could be anything from a joke to a scandal. My daddy, when in the mood, could tease her gently about it. When my mother was a child, her mother had a life that was extremely hard. She might well have been a freed slave, but she had no rights in the matter. But my mother, Mary, never felt anything but compassion and pride for her mother and her plight. She never made excuse for her, never felt she had to, never showed even a trace of shame as some people might have.

My mother would say, "My poor mother, she didn't know any better. She just had a hard life." There was love and appreciation, a deep, abiding pride in what her mother had accomplished. She knew the story, and she also knew her mother had worked very hard within the social strictures of the day, under which, where out-of-wedlock children were concerned, she had none of the power and all the responsibility.

Children of black-white unions were common enough. Under the unstated "one-drop rule" of Southern life—indeed, of US life, right down to the present moment—my mother was half-black and, therefore, all black. You can still see this

6

kind of reasoning today. After all, President Barack Obama, son of a black father and a white mother, is regularly called the first black president, and his white ancestry is much less in the foreground of the way people talk about him. There were many terms for such children—*half-breed* or *bastard child*. Such an origin guaranteed that child a betwixt and between life, having to fight for acceptance or endure comments or jokes.

It was a common saying that "among our people, nobody was a purebred." Just by looking at faces, you could tell white men were part of many people's ancestry. White men did, because they could, take advantage of black women and got away with it. It was next to impossible to prosecute such rapes in court and next to impossible to get unwilling white fathers to support children begotten of unions with black women. Some such children went on to pass for white. Others became "high yaller" gals, accorded social status in the black community because of their lighter skin. As mentioned, my daddy's family was very dark, and there were some on that side who would not easily accept my mother because of her skin color and origins. Much of it was just envy over her lighter skin.

Thank God she was the woman she was and won most of them over eventually.

When my mother got to school-age, her father took an active interest in her education. He could easily have cast his unacknowledged children aside, but to his credit, he wanted Mother to achieve and have as much chance at a good life as she could. He did not want her to attend the traditional black schools in Fayette, so he sent mother to live with his sister and her children in New Orleans.

She was accepted in this household and treated kindly. She grew up in a white household with many of the conveniences and privileges of a white girl. Mother did not, however, have the same education as her white cousins. Every day, those cousins got on the bus to elementary school. Then a black woman would come to the house and teach my mother in the kitchen. These were serious lessons meant to educate my mother to school standards. You could think of it as an early example of homeschooling.

Once my mother completed her elementary school education, her father sent her to that all-girls preparatory boarding school in Meridian, a town closer to Fayette than it was from Greenwood. This school had many mixed-race students born under circumstances like my mother's.

My daddy and mother's lives had begun to run in parallel. Daddy was attending the boys' prep near my mother's school. They met and began dating, which was far different from dating today: almost never alone, extremely decorous and observant of the moral boundaries of the time. Plus, there was an age difference: daddy was older than my mother. He would graduate from his prep school much before mother would from hers. But before he graduated and went off to college, he and my mother agreed that after he completed his college degree, they would wed.

Daddy applied and was accepted to Philander Smith College, a black college in Little Rock, Arkansas. The college had originally been instituted to offer education to freed slaves. He excelled in school and was interested in medicine. He was also a pretty good pitcher on their baseball team. He would graduate in four years with a liberal arts bachelor's degree. He applied to Meharry Medical College in Nashville, Tennessee, with the promise of a scholarship. Fate intervened, however. My father's parents had passed away, and authority over their property and affairs had passed to an older brother who refused the scholarship on daddy's behalf, something my daddy would resent for the rest of his life.

In the meantime, my mother stayed at the boarding school, graduated, and got a scholarship in home economics to attend Knoxville College in Knoxville, Tennessee. She was yet another example of how black or mixed-race students found ways forward thanks to scholarships. Like Philander Smith, Knoxville began as a school to educate freed slaves. Part of a small entering class of six women, she entered Knoxville in 1917, the same year the United States joined World War I.

At first, the country tried a volunteer system of getting enlistments, but that didn't work. So the Selective Service Act of 1917 was passed, and Daddy was drafted. He went into training for a year. In fact, he was in New York, preparing to ship overseas to serve, when word came on November 11, 1918, that the war had ended. My daddy often told me later that God had answered his prayers because, all throughout that very day, he had prayed repeatedly that the war would end and he would not have to travel to Europe to fight.

Daddy notified my mother that they were now free to marry as they had agreed to a few years before. Things were like that then. Today, engagements can be pretty short, and it's rare to encounter a scenario in which a couple's promise to marry actually results in getting married as promised. Such scenarios were far from rare back in 1917. I suspect they might have been somewhat more common among some African American communities. Weddings often were deferred for a long time as the prospective couple looked for ways to make a living and save a little bit before starting off into the world together. That often meant traveling to where the work was, undergoing hardships, and trying to save out of miserable wages. Sometimes, as it almost did in my daddy's case, it meant going off to war, or at least training for it. My mother and daddy spent years hundreds of miles apart, rarely seeing each other. And I imagine that my mother, down there in Knoxville College, must have worried herself, terribly worried, over my daddy's fate as he prepared for whatever war would bring. But these two were hardly alone. Life was different then.

That was quite a promise. My mother left Knoxville and gave her home economics scholarship to a cousin; many such scholarships of the time were "portable" in this fashion. My parents got married on that September day in

1919 in the Nero Chapel outside Greenwood, on cousin Willis Nero's land. One generation away from slavery, they brought together Choctaw, white, and African bloodlines, and they went off to make what life they could on good cotton-growing land.

On my father's land, he and his brothers had built a one-bedroom house with a kitchen, a living room, and a dining room. Like many such houses, it had a corrugated tin roof that magnified the heat of the summer sun and turned any rainstorm into an unholy racket. The house was leaky, drafty, and jerry-built, but it was home. That was where they settled down and began their family.

This role, while it gave her much of the pride and happiness she would know in life, resulted initially in heartbreak. My mother would give birth to seven live children and one stillborn child, with one birth about every two years. Three of her first four children would not survive infancy. The first child was named Myrtle. She died young from a disease the doctor thought might be polio, although this was never a certain diagnosis. The next child was named Florene. She lived to eighteen months, an energetic, curious little toddler. My mother and daddy kept her in a crib in the yard while they were out working in the fields. One day, Florene somehow got out of the crib, and while wandering around, she happened to see a neighbor boy of ours, mentally challenged, who was walking down the road. Florene toddled after him, and when he crossed a bridge over a lake, the little baby followed, lost her balance, fell in, and drowned. In 1924, my brother David M. Nero Jr. was born next, and then a son, John Stark, who was stillborn.

In the 1920s, Mississippi had the highest maternal and infant mortality rates in the country. The rate was higher for black children than for white. In 1940, just three years after I was born, the infant mortality rate in Mississippi among blacks was 60.9 per 1,000 live births, compared to 46.3 for whites. Medical care was poor, and malnourishment and infectious diseases struck many families. But those statistics, as jaw-dropping as they are, mask the grief that struck thousands of parents who lost children. We are accustomed to think that such grief is perhaps the worst a person can endure. Well, multiply that grief by thousands throughout Mississippi. Make it a fact of life for family after family. The enormity of it surpasses understanding.

Such was the trauma that descended on Mother and Daddy. The farm had to keep going: my mother was back in the fields soon after she gave birth, whether the children lived or died. Growing up, of course, I heard about my sisters Myrtle and Florene and of my brother John Stark, but the way they were spoken of told me of a suffering beyond words.

The first child to live a full life, David M. Nero Jr., would do us all proud, going on to succeed in the armed forces and in business. After him came son Clyde and daughters Colleen and Mary Jean, whom we called Jean. I was a surprise, born after a lag of about five years, when my mother was almost forty and my father, fifty. Because of complications arising perhaps from the age of the mother, I was the only child in my whole family to be born in a hospital.

## A Family Working Together

Greenwood was at one time called the cotton capital of the South. It is set amid the Mississippi Delta land, very fertile, flat, hot, and humid, all ideal for the growth and harvesting of cotton. We lived and worked in the midst of that land, and when I was a child, cotton was still an important cash crop. American textile mills still led the world—textile manufacturing had not yet migrated to Asia—and so cotton was still in crucial demand, and its farming and harvesting still represented an important livelihood in the Southern states.

Our dilapidated house was where we grew up. We thought of it as home and never considered ourselves different, exceptional, heroic, or anything. We were like kids everywhere: we'd rather not work if we could get out of it—only, this being a working farm, we couldn't get out of it. The rhythms of work were the rhythms of our early lives.

On Daddy's fifty-one acres, we would farm about twenty acres of cotton and ten acres of corn. The rest was where the house sat, a large garden, the pasturelands for the animals, and the woods. Our house had no indoor plumbing. We had a sink, an outdoor pump, with an outhouse. We did not have indoor electric service for much of my childhood. We heated the house by wood fire in the kitchen, and we had an icebox rather than a refrigerator. We did our homework and reading by a single large kerosene lamp, which we shared. Our parents utilized another lamp for reading the Bible to the family. When I reached middle school, in the late 1940s, Daddy had the house wired for electricity, which consisted of a single outlet. We ran a cord for an electric light. Daddy also bought a battery-powered radio, on which we listened to many of the most popular radio serials of the day. It was the age of radio, and although we didn't always have the clearest signal, it brought us information and thrills.

You had to be resourceful, and our parents were. Just for an example— toothbrushes. They just weren't plentiful. They cost money, buying them meant a trip to town and back, and they were simply the kind of thing we didn't have until much later. At the farm, mother used to break off twigs and use a penknife to pare them down and then run the penknife down the side to feather them and create bristles, and we'd use that as our toothbrush. Instead of toothpaste, we used baking soda or salt. Those were just little things, but they indicated how we lived. You can bet we got new clothes very seldom, maybe once a year, or when hand-me-downs came from relatives whose children had outgrown them. We were part of a network of families who mailed used clothes around to the relatives who needed them. Such "care packages" crisscrossed the South, thousands and thousands, just one more way generations came up together.

We had horses to pull our wagon and plow, and we also had dairy cows. The milk and buttermilk we drank, and the butter was for our cooking and food. We also kept chickens for eggs and meat. In the earlier years, we raised our own hogs, but later, it became more convenient to buy our pork from butchers, and I don't think we much missed the hog-tending. Many of our chores revolved around these crucial animals, which grazed in the large pasture. In the woods, we could cut down the fuel we needed for cooking and heating. We had one large garden, in which we grew tomatoes, okra, beans, carrots, beets, cabbages, and collards. We also kept two smaller, separate plots, on which we grew peanuts, potatoes, and sweet potatoes. We ate fresh vegetables in season, and mother would put up a lot of vegetables and fruits in jars for the winter months.

We didn't have motorized tractors, or even a truck, until I was in high school. We did everything by hand or with the aid of animals. But we were nearing the end of that world, until mechanized means of harvesting took the place of human workers. As history shows, the induction of machines spurred a mass exodus of African Americans to the cities of the North and the Northeast. There wasn't much else to do around Greenwood unless your ambition was to be a schoolteacher, janitor, or domestic worker. Most of my classmates and their families left after high school. They went to places like Detroit, Chicago, New York, or Los Angeles to get better jobs. My siblings and I would be part of that picture.

The farm was dedicated to growing cotton. Five days a week, that was what our parents did, with assistance from other hired workers, plus the help of the kids when we got home from school. When school was out for the summer, we were expected to be in the fields all together, all day. On Saturdays, we had laundry and cleaning to do as well as animal chores. On Sundays, we milked the cows and did some light morning chores, but no work in the fields. It was the Lord's Day. My parents were Christians and tried very hard to live by the Bible and get us to do the same. We attended the Wesley Methodist Church and eventually Decell Methodist Church in Greenwood when we could get there. We were three miles outside of town, a good walk or horse-drawn trip. Sundays was also the day of our wonderful Sunday meal.

I'm not going to tell you that as kids, we loved getting out in the fields and working in the unrelenting heat. We disliked it, even dreaded the work sometimes. We understood, though, that this was how it was, and we knew the importance of working hard, of being organized, punctual, detail-oriented, and of completing the chore you were assigned. We lived within the natural rhythm of growth, maturation, and harvest. We worked alongside our parents in the common task. In some ways, I guess, I was lucky to be the youngest. My siblings did more than I. They taught me how to do my job and made sure I did it well.

On weekends and when school was out, we had a full day of serious toil, working sunup to sundown. When I was about seven or eight, and Mary Jean was twelve or thirteen, we'd be in the fields by six and work until noon. Colleen and I would then go back to the house at around ten and make a fire for cooking in the wood-burning stove. I'd churn the milk to make butter and buttermilk to drink, and Colleen, a better cook than Mary Jean, would make our midday meal, called dinner. She'd make enough for both dinner and supper because we didn't want to make a second fire during the summer. It would have heated the house again and made it pretty much impossible to sleep.

At noon, everybody came to the house, and we'd all eat. In thirty minutes, we were finished, and the dishes were washed. Mother and Daddy would take a nap, and the girls would go off on their various pursuits. My friend Glen, a little white kid who lived up the road, might come over, and we, like any eight-year-olds, would be out running around, catching grasshoppers and playing. We could kick up a lot of noise, and that would make my sisters pretty angry: it could wake Mother up before they wanted her to. Because when Mother woke up, it was time for all of us to get back to the fields and work. So my sisters wanted Mother to have a good, long nap.

One of my earliest memories of farmwork is of carrying water to my family as they worked in the fields. I might have been too small to work in the field, but I still had chores to do. I started picking cotton with the family by the time I was seven, and I continued until I started tenth grade. By the time I was ten or eleven, I was big, strong, and responsible enough to use a sharp hoe for cotton-chopping. I was big enough to do all the chores that needed to be done.

Cotton farming was hard work. First, you had to prepare the ground and plant the cotton. Daddy did most of that. He was the one who turned the soil over by horse-drawn plow. In the springtime, we would do what was called chopping the cotton. We would take hoes and chop the grass and weeds from between the stalks to keep the grass from consuming valuable nutrients from the cotton. This was grueling work, and we would get tired, and the hoe would lose its edge. My brother Clyde, the only older boy still at home by then, had the unenviable task of sharpening the hoes, which he had to do twice a day, so they'd keep their edge and allow us to cut the grass in easier sweeps.

We would chop the cotton three separate times before it was ready to be picked. There was a time of waiting, and the cotton stalks would grow a beautiful dark green, and there would be pink, red, white, and yellow blooms. You could look across the cotton field, and it would be a beautiful scene.

Those blooms were the precursors to the cotton locks. When the blooms fell off, it meant the bolls were ready to open. When they did, they would reveal the white cotton fibers ready, exposed and ready to be picked. The cotton bolls didn't open up all at one time. There'd be a series of openings: some bolls opened right away, some later, and some younger and less mature plants would not open until weeks later. So harvesttime sprawled across the summer. We would plant the cotton in March or April. We'd start picking cotton as early as July, really get into it in August, and likely finish up with a final round of harvesting in mid-September. You'd pick all the cotton you could find, pull the locks off the bolls, stuff the locks in a sack until you couldn't stuff in any more, then carry the sack on your back to the scale, weigh it, and then empty it into the wagon. We'd keep doing this as long as there was daylight. Daddy would take the cotton in the wagon to the gin and get it processed.

This whole process would be repeated weeks later a second time, for the bolls that had opened later. We worked back through the fields again, picking, stuffing, lugging the sacks to the scale, emptying them into the wagon, and getting back out to the fields. And then maybe, there would be a third and final time, when you would go through the fields and pick the latest bolls to open, and then you were finished for the year.

The cotton gin separated the seed of the cotton from the fiber locks. You could save the seed for your own use, or you could sell it. The locks, the commercially indispensable part, were put in bales. Usually, you wanted your final bale to be about one-third of the weight of all the cotton you had picked. We'd shoot for about 1,500 pounds of cotton from the fields. At that time, the sale rate was about thirty to thirty-two cents a pound, so a five-hundred-pound load of cotton would yield about $150, a lot of money in those days. That would pay for school clothes, food, electric bills, and it also paid the field-workers. We kept a record of how much their sacks weighed. They were paid about $1.50 to $2.00 per one hundred pounds picked.

Daddy had a little family ritual on his way home from the gin. He would always stop at the local store and buy us peppermint candies and grapes. My siblings and I could not wait for him to get home with them. When he came home, Mother would ask, "Honey, how much did it weigh?"

My daddy's answer was "Five hundred pounds!"

Daddy also grew corn, both for the table and for the farm animals. We would plant the corn in March, and it would be ready to eat in June or July. That was the "early corn," for us to eat. The rest of the corn would stay out there to dry up. In August and September, my dad would pull up the dried-up corn and put it into several heaps. When the kids came from school, we would hitch the wagon and take it to the barn to feed chickens, horses, and cows.

By 1945, I was eight years old, and World War II was still happening. There were four children still on the Nero farm: brother Clyde, sisters Colleen and Mary Jean, and me. We'd get up early and see to our chores. We had to cut wood for our stove and keep lots of fresh wood in readiness. There were cows to be milked.

My brother Clyde and I would get up, milk the cows, then go back in and take a bath. We didn't want to smell like cows all day.

In wintertime, the oldest boy in the house also had the important duty of getting up in the early darkness and lighting the fire in the woodstove so the house would be warm when we all got up and Mother could cook breakfast. We would get up unwillingly in a winter-cold house and feel our way in the freezing dark to the stove, put in the wood, light it, get the fire going, bank it, close the grate, and then hop back in bed for a half-hour more sleep.

The kids would begin chores for an hour or more before it was time to have breakfast: biscuits, eggs, some kind of meat (such as bacon or sausage), plus sometimes pancakes or even spoon bread, a rich, filling cornmeal-based side dish. We also had sorghum molasses to accompany our biscuits. Then we would go to school. Mother and Daddy worked all day in the fields while we were at school. On school days, we'd go straight home, change, have something to eat, and get out into the fields, where we would work until sundown. Then came supper and homework.

If we were chopping cotton, all of us would walk out to the fields with a hoe on our shoulders. Everybody had a row. When I got older, I had my own row too. So five of us were each responsible for a row with two to three other helpers, and daddy was doing the plowing with the animals.

When we got to the end of our row, sometimes we would end up at the shade trees. My sister Mary Jean would play this game where she would work the fastest and get to the shade first and look back from underneath the shade at the rest of us still working in the hot sun. She could work pretty rapidly.

It was difficult work, but it was what we knew. We had it much better than the sharecroppers. They lived and worked on someone else's farm, and they didn't have the kind of options we had. In most cases, for example, the owners of the land told them if and when the kids could go to school. Our parents, as I've discussed, weren't going to let anything get in the way of our education. When school was out, we worked pretty hard, sunup to sundown. When school started, our parents sent us to school, and they worked the fields with other people, and when we came home from school, we changed clothes, got a bite to eat, and then went out and worked until the sun went down. Then we did our homework by kerosene lamp, took a bath, and slept very well.

My daddy and mother would have told you with confidence that all of us worked hard, but some of us did it with better will than others. As mentioned, when I was born, my mother was forty years old and my daddy was fifty. So I saw them in the declining years of their lives, still farming every daylight hour of every day. By the time I was in tenth grade, my parents rented out the farm, and I would work for the renter on weekends. I was often the one doing a lot of the heavy lifting. I seldom made a fuss. Our parents used to say that Colleen and I were good because we never complained, while Mary Jean and Clyde were complainers. From the very beginning, as a little boy, I displayed a readiness to do what I was told. That was because my siblings were making sure I knew what to do and did it. But it was also this: I knew that if I didn't do it, my daddy or mother would have to do it. So I accepted that responsibility.

## Boys and Girls, Men and Women

My mother and sisters did everything around the farm. I have spoken of things Clyde or I would usually do, such as chopping wood, making fires, milking cows, and cleaning the yard. My mother and sisters were good hands at all of them and would do them if necessary. My sisters worked alongside the men. Our family farm was both a place of daily roles you had to play and an equality of responsibility and labor. That steadiness and togetherness were two more strokes of luck for me.

I had several conversations with my father about the place of women in the family and, in a larger sense, in African American life. He always had a great deal of respect for black women. He felt black women had saved the black race because even though many black women could have chosen not to do so, many of them stayed in the families they had chosen, showed loyalty, commitment, and perseverance, and did many things very helpful to our race. Daddy knew mother was the glue of our family, and he was always proud of her. He knew how hard he expected her to work, and he knew how onerous the roles and duties of cook, farmer, child bearer, and housekeeper were on her or on any woman. Yet he also knew that, in owning their own house and land and working together, they had it better than many other black families in which the husband might farm while the wife might leave the house and work in a white household.

"Let's say you're an itinerant farmer or a sharecropper," Daddy would say, "and the wife is a cook, babysitter, or housekeeper. The husband is the farmer, taking care of the animals and picking the cotton. Now the mother goes to the big house, the home of the owner of the land, in her white dress and white shoes, to take care of the baby, cook, and so forth. The white husband of the family leaves the house in the morning and kisses his wife good-bye. The black woman watches this and is going to be there all day, taking care of this couple's children. Then she goes back home, and her husband comes back from the fields and the animals, dirty, sweaty. He smells like the animals, and she might look around and say, 'There's nothing this man can do for me. If he can't provide for me better than this . . .'"

But many black women didn't do that. They supported their husbands and families and hung in there under often-harsh circumstances. My father saluted them for their hard work and the cohesion they brought to families and society.

## The Value of a Busy Day

Think about how organized we had to be, especially on a school day. We were up at 4:30 a.m., did chores, bathed, got a hot breakfast courtesy of Mother, and were off to school by six. We had a three-mile walk into Greenwood to get to school—no school bus for black kids. Our white neighbors sometimes would wave to us from the bus as it passed us by. Sometimes we could get a lift about halfway home, not from native-born white folks, but sometimes from a burly Swedish man named Alex Granholm, who knew how things were and felt fine giving us a ride partway if he saw us on the road. At 3:30 p.m., we were out of school and on the three-mile road home.

As an adult, I eventually would gravitate to the field of dentistry and orthodontics, in which you must be observant, reliable, and methodical, with a human touch. You can't be afraid of hard, physical work either. That was never something I ever had the luxury of being afraid of. The farming life, with its daily regularity, its demanding, sometimes-backbreaking schedule, made all of us reliable, steady, hardworking people. We were people with not a lot of spare time. We applied the same virtues to our schoolwork.

## Why None of Us Became Farmers

Once, when I was a graduate student at the University of Kentucky College of Dentistry, I talked with my adviser, Dr. Sheldon Rovin. He asked me about my father and family, and I said something like "My dad was not as aggressive as he could have been with the farm. He could have done this and that, he could have had a better house" and so on.

Dr. Rovin stopped me, and he said, "Let me tell you something: You have no idea what your father was going through down there in Mississippi as a black man. I imagine he always had a lot on his mind. He probably always had a lot of loans, like almost any farmer, so many years he was almost dying with anxiety when he had to get more loans to get back in line again." He was absolutely right. I never again said anything like that about my daddy again.

To make a farm succeed, a farmer has to be more than just a tiller of the soil. He has to be equal parts botanist, animal scientist, and magician. He has to be the boss of a team. He has to have a payroll. He has to be a businessman and make sure he gets paid fairly for his products. He has to work with banks, perhaps with bankers who are reluctant to lend to him in early-twentieth-century Mississippi. And he has to have superhuman patience, self-reliance, hope, and a bale of luck. That's on top of being a good man, father, husband, and neighbor. My daddy did a fine job of all those.

He and Mother taught us what we had to do to survive. They wanted us to go to college, get educated, and have good jobs. They saw how things were for black people in many ways spoken and unspoken. They raised us to be courteous and cautious at the same time, and they probably saw that things were changing rapidly. When black soldiers came home from World War II, thousands of them returned with expanded horizons and expectations. Thanks to Harry S. Truman, the army became the first sector of US society to become integrated by law. At the end of the 1940s, that development foretold the next three decades of social change and protest. Meanwhile, mechanization was steadily destroying the old ways in Mississippi, prompting thousands of African Americans to search for better work and opportunities. Our parents pressed us to do well in school, and we pressed one another to do well in both positive and not-so-positive ways.

Why all this stress on achievement? Because they didn't want us to stay where we were. That's the loving irony of my upbringing: the farming life taught me I would someday leave the farm.

# CHAPTER 2

## NEIGHBORS, TOWN, CLASSMATES

I am going to save a more detailed discussion of race for the next chapter, but the "facts" of race, "the way it was" as we were taught and understood it, stood large and clear in the background, distinct yet unspoken, in much of what we did. That includes our relations with our neighbors.

We were three miles out of town, as I've mentioned, and the 1930s and 1940s in agricultural Mississippi were a time when three miles was a good, definitive distance: once you were not in town, you were quickly in the country. So we didn't have much of what you might call a neighborhood. There were, in our vicinity, four households: ours; another black family, who generally were transient; and two white families, the Connerlys and the Bufords. Both families lived on land, it's interesting to note, once owned by my paternal grandfather, John Tyler Nero.

The Connerlys owned their land and were farmers. Mr. Alcus Connerly had been a switchman on a freight train before turning to farming. He and his wife, Katie Betts, had high school educations. They had three children: Susan, who was older and out of the house; Nell, who became a good friend of mine; and Teddy, who couldn't hear or speak.

The Bufords lived as sharecroppers; they had little education. The father, Brooks, was also a cattle dealer and liked to bid on cattle at local auctions. His son was named George Glen, but we always knew him as Glen. He was probably my best friend growing up. They also had three girls, Margie, Ina Jean, and Nancy. The Bufords also included George Buford, the grandfather. He liked nothing more than to come over, which he often did, and sit on the porch and talk to Daddy for hours. I can still hear Mr. Buford now, arguing a point by crying out good-naturedly, "I *know*! I study human nature!" That was Mr. Buford.

These two white families lived about a quarter of a mile on either side of us. They didn't like each other very much, but each white family liked us just fine, within the rules. As mentioned, the Connerlys had some schooling, but the Bufords had little. The Connerlys looked down on the Bufords as lower class; the Bufords saw the Connerlys as uppity. The children of both families would come over to our house, in the middle, all the time. They often played or did homework with us. But the Bufords would never let their children play with the Connerlys, nor would the Connerlys let their kid play with the Bufords.

My daddy ran a family cotton farm. He was a farmer and was out in the fields every day, working, as he had been raised to work, as hard as he could to make his fields work for him. *Prosperous* probably isn't the exact word for the results, but *respectable* certainly is. It was a robust business. He and Mother were able to raise a good family and send them to college. And my daddy eventually was able to pay off every note on his farm. I remind you of all this because, on the face of it, you'd think Daddy might have pride of place among his neighbors. The neighbors did respect and like him. I have many memories of one of the adults from one of the families coming over and sitting in front with Daddy to talk about almost anything or of one of the mothers coming over to talk to my mother. As you'll see, mother was, in many ways, the mediator of disputes and, thus, the cohering force of our tiny neighborhood.

As mentioned, the Connerlys and the Bufords liked us Neros just fine. But they disliked one another. An immemorial, stubborn class resentment arose between two families that otherwise really weren't that different. That led to some complicated and interesting relationships. We became the peacemakers on our road. Blacks as peacemakers among white folks—how about that?

We knew that the relationships were complicated. Glen Buford was a good friend and playmate of mine, and we used to play together in the fields and also accompany his daddy, Brooks Buford, or my daddy when they ran errands. We played all the games of boyhood. We played baseball and football in the fields, often disrupting my parents' midday nap, and we caught grasshoppers and put "saddles" and "reins" made of string on them. This is cruel but perhaps interesting: we used to pull off their hoppers and tie threads to them and make them pull little matchbooks, which would be their wagons. We'd pretend we had adjacent farms, and big tree root was the border between Glen's farm and mine. And the grasshoppers would pull the tractors around, and we'd make up stories about farming. And we had little thought for the difference in skin color. When you're a kid out playing, you're a kid out playing, and all you want to do is play, and that's what you do. It's sweet to think about how all the other stuff just falls away and kids just want to be kids. The bad social dynamics lock back in place, sadly, in other situations. We could never have gone to the same schools. His schools were not open to me, and he would never have been sent to mine. As far as the larger society in Mississippi or the South was concerned, we lived in separate universes and had very different outlooks.

I like to think of myself and Glen playing catch or raising hell without a care in the world. That's the way it should have been right then for two little guys out in the field on a Sunday afternoon. And that was the way it often was.

The white children were allowed to come to our house, and they often did. Glen used to eat at our house and, sometimes, even sleep over. Nell Connerly used to come over constantly. But we were not allowed to take the same liberties and go over to their houses. If we ever did, and I can't recall it happening too often, we would have had to enter by the back door. That was just how it was. But we were never to eat at their houses or sleep over. They would not have had us nor would we have wanted to go.

I remember sister Colleen helping out Nell Connerly with her homework. In our house we had a firm system whereby the older children helped the youngsters with their studies, sometimes literally looking over their shoulders with techniques ranging from gentle care to teasing, encouraging, and demanding that the youngsters do well. They scrutinized the younger kids' work, almost as surrogate parents—in fact, in those instances, exactly as surrogate parents. If I lagged in one class or brought home marks that were a little off, I'd be sure to hear it from somebody and get help when somebody thought I needed it. It spurred me to work as hard as I could. The house had high standards; my daddy and mother's expectations stood before and behind everything we did or expected of ourselves. I'm not going to tell you we were never lazy or never misbehaved or complained. What I am suggesting, though, is that our little family system did sustain each child as he or she came up. Everyone played a role consciously in the act of upholding the child, instructing, encouraging, correcting.

Many families work like this; much of the time, that's what family is, isn't it? And the child from a family like that, whatever his or her natural skills and talents may be, has a big advantage over the child who has no such family, or a broken family, or a family unwilling to uphold and sustain that child.

That was yet another of my lucky breaks, having the brothers and sisters I had.

The Nero kids, I think, got something of a reputation for being good in school. So maybe it was no surprise that when Nell Connerly, or one of the white children, had difficulty in a class, she appeared on our doorstep, and Colleen might look at her work and sit down with her and help. I doubt Colleen uttered a single complaint. Her role was to sit down and help, and she did that just as she did with me and just as another sibling had done with her. This fit right into the way our family operated.

I know I have mentioned that my mother was a fantastic cook, a talent she passed on to Colleen. My mother was especially in her pride on holidays such as Thanksgiving and Christmas, when we'd have friends and relatives come from all around. She'd make dozens of pies ahead of time, those that would keep, and she made the table groan with the epic, delicious meals she'd produce. Every Christmas, it was her particular concern to repaint the kitchen. Smoke and soot from our wood-burning stove blackened the walls during the year, and for the holiday season, she made a point of giving the whole kitchen a coat of fresh paint. We joined willingly in the repainting since it was a sign of the approaching holidays and it was for mother. Still today, the smell of fresh paint brings a smile to my lips because it is laden with happy memories of home and Christmas.

Sundays saw our big family meal, an oversize country dinner, in which mother took great pride. She always cooked more than enough. She did that in general because a farming family is a hungry family, and one of us was always hunting around in the icebox for a snack. In summer, too, we tried to use the stove as sparingly as possible so as not to heat the house too often. Many meals were stretched across days.

But there was another reason our Sunday dinners were as big as they were. Most of our guests were black neighbors who had walked, many of them for miles, from parts far and near to sit and eat with us. They'd show up at about one o'clock; that was when we usually ate. Once they had left, though, one or another of our white neighbor families would show up, hoping for some leftovers, which there always were. Mr. Brooks Buford especially loved my mother's homemade rolls: "Mary, do you have any more of those rolls? I never tasted anything as good as those damn rolls in my life."

They'd just kind of materialize. Places could always be found for company, and they would be made welcome. Our cousins would come from town and grumble sometimes about the white neighbors praying and eating with us, but Mother and Daddy always insisted that their welcome extended to all. Our white neighbors had to walk only about a quarter mile to get to our porch, but I got the impression that, for a taste of mother's good cooking, they'd have walked several times that distance.

The cooking was very, very good. For drinks, there would be sweet ice tea or lemonade. Then came the famous homemade rolls, string beans, butter beans, corn, okra, and tomato salad. The entrée would be one or sometimes two meats, such as roast beef or, our very favorite, stewed chicken and dumplings, the thought of which makes my mouth water to this very day. And dessert would usually be some kind of cobbler. My daddy did not like cake, but he did like his cobbler, blackberry or apple.

My parents were congenial hosts, and talk around the table was free and familial, with compliments and jokes plus abundant thanks to the cook. My daddy was the one who'd keep everyone laughing. As a hardworking man, he enjoyed what little leisure time he had, and he liked company. Everyone ate heartily, as mother expected, and she had the pride of the pantry.

When all the courses had been passed and the last of the dessert had been demolished, our guests would thank us and take their leave. As kids, we were upset because now we had dishes to do. The kids did the dishes in our house, especially on this big-eating day. Sunday dishes were a big job, and when one or another of our neighbor families showed up, that would about double the amount.

From time to time, one family would aid another. When I foolishly set fire to the fields near our house, the Buford family came running with water in pots and pans.

Tensions sometimes boiled up, revealing the potential for real trouble always beneath the surface in race relations in those days. Mother handled such situations with grace and patience. She had the knack of being able to talk to anybody. Her skills, I hope, rubbed off on me. They certainly helped me later when I was the only black person in an overwhelmingly white environment of college and professional advanced education. People later told me I had patience, panache, and understanding.

## Town

Stepping back, I can say my family was busy, committed, and somewhat isolated. Those three miles from town were an effective buffer, for better or worse. With the constant demands of farming life, we had little time to have friends from school over. Later, when I was school-age, I rarely brought friends home partly because of the distance they'd have to travel to get to our house and then back home and, later in high school, partly because I didn't want my town friends to see our house, which Daddy and his brothers had built and which was seldom, if ever, improved or repaired. It goes a little too far to say I was ashamed of it, but I really would rather not have them see how we lived.

Mother seldom went to town, except for two or three times a year, when she bought school clothes for us and a thing or two for herself. Daddy took the wagon into town several times a week. He did most of the food shopping for the family, getting our greens and meat and other food. He also checked the family's hallowed post office box. John Tyler Nero, my grandfather, had opened PO Box 363 in the 1890s, and of the brothers, my daddy was in and around Greenwood the most, so he took over the box. The family still has this box to this day. With the Neros and their relatives now spread out over the country, I'm sure some of my younger relatives will be asking someday what we should do with it. I'll hate to see it go. But in the late 1930s and through the 1950s, that PO Box would be the conduit for Daddy's business correspondence, orders of farm equipment and seed catalogues, and mail from family.

# School

*low expectations)*

As black children in the Mississippi in the first half of the twentieth century, we were regarded by the wider society as nothing and were expected to achieve nothing. That's clear as I sit here now, and from time to time, it was clear to me back then. It's also true, however, that as a kid growing up, I was focused on the things of my life, my very full, very meaningful life in the bosom of a hardworking, supportive, demanding family who got me pointed in the right direction. So I did not really dwell on the injustices in the wider society around me. Nor did my classmates in school. But we all knew about them. People saw us as nothing and expected nothing from us.

We were seeing signs that things might someday be different. As of my 1956 graduation, we were just beginning to see African Americans of achievement take the world stage. Yes, in entertainment we'd had quite a few already, with Louis Armstrong, Duke Ellington, Billie Holiday, Coleman Hawkins, Art Tatum, Nat King Cole, and so many others. With Jackie Robinson, Larry Doby, Kenny Washington, Woody Strode, and Earl Lloyd, the walls had started, piecemeal, to crumble in baseball, football, and basketball. The summer I graduated, a student a couple of years behind me actually competed in the Melbourne Olympics and won a silver medal in the long jump, the first US woman ever to medal in that event. That would be Willye B. White, who was born in Money, Mississippi, grew up on a sharecropper's farm picking cotton, and eventually attended Broad Street High with me.

*graduated*

Still, it was a world in which little was expected of us, a world we, in turn, *30 college* could expect to be very hard and resistant. But look at what happened. Out of the *49* forty-nine graduating members of my all-black class of 1956 from Broad Street High School, thirty fully went on to graduate from college. At least three of the women went on to be registered nurses. At least ten of us went on to earn advanced degrees in education and become schoolteachers. My good friend Alma Green Henderson went to Tougaloo College and stayed in Mississippi and became a teacher. That was a route my older brother Clyde would follow, returning to Stone Street as a teacher and principal. Grace Dillard got her master's in social work at the University of Pennsylvania. One classmate, Joanne Hammonds, earned a PhD in bacteriology from Smith College and went on to teach at Meharry Medical College in Nashville, Tennessee. I actually took Joanne to our high school prom. She is a gracious and extraordinarily gifted person.

I went from a farm in Mississippi to become a successful orthodontist in one of the largest practices in Philadelphia, certainly one of the very few black men at that time even to become orthodontists. My good friend Alexander Scott was a prominent business leader and a regional director of the Boy Scouts in Mississippi. His father had a massive farm about thirty miles from Greenwood, and when Alexander retired, he went back to the farm. My close friend Charles Blackmon went on to earn an MBA at Wake Forest University. In 1962, he became a computer programmer for the North Carolina Mutual Life Insurance Company, working his way up the ranks eventually to become senior vice president. He held many civil and professional posts, including chairman of the board of trustees of Durham County Hospital in North Carolina, also serving in the board of trustees of Duke University Health System.

Then there is Morgan Freeman. He graduated a year ahead of me at Broad Street, in 1955. He had distinguished himself as an actor since the age of twelve, when he won a big statewide drama competition. While still in high school, Morgan acted in a radio show that originated in Nashville. He was already acting when he came to Broad Street. But I knew him best as the drum major of the marching band and a very good friend. He was in the glee club and the debating team also. He helped Broad Street High School win the state drama title in 1951, 1952, and 1954. He did all these things even though he was often chronically undernourished, a condition that nearly led to his death by drowning when he, while swimming in a lake, ran out of energy and sank like a stone. He had to be rescued by the other kids. Morgan had a tough way up. His parents sent him as a baby to live with a grandmother in Charleston, Mississippi, and he was moved around a lot as a child.

But look what Morgan has achieved. He's one of the most famous actors— indeed one of the most recognizable faces and voices—in the whole world. He has won all sorts of awards, including an Academy Award in 2005 for Supporting Actor in the film *Million Dollar Baby*. He's been nominated a couple of times for Best Actor, and I can't figure out why he hasn't won a couple of those awards yet.

He has often credited our great drama teacher, Mrs. Leola Gregory Williams, with changing his life. I might add that Mrs. Williams changed a lot of lives, including mine. She caught him flirting with girls, cried "Morgan, you about a mess!" and got him to take up drama to burn off his excess of high spirits. And the rest is history.

We had to leave Greenwood to achieve these things; that much was clear. These days, when my classmates and I assemble, now in our seventies, we reflect on the many ways our high school oriented us. It allowed us to do things for ourselves in a world where no one else was going to come and do them for us.

No matter how you look at it, this high school, like this group of students, was very special. It is amazing what we ended up accomplishing. We had, in the American way of things, next to no prospects.

Each of these children had a story before he or she came to school, and I didn't know all of them. Some had excellent families who, like mine, sustained them and expected good things from them. But many did not. Many, like Morgan

Freeman, had already experienced the rootless, chaotic life sometimes imposed on the young black mind and soul. We were a diverse group.

What we had in common, starting in high school, were some of the most devoted teachers we could have hoped for. Scan the pages of the 1956 edition of the *Tiger*, our school yearbook, and you'll see photographs of teachers working with students. My copy contains inscriptions from beloved teachers.

The four teachers who made a huge difference in my life were the aforementioned Mrs. Williams, English and drama teacher; Mrs. O. W. Perry, English and debate teacher; and two coaches, Mr. Charles Leonard, who coached football and basketball and later went off to dental school at Meharry, and Mr. Paul Thomas, coach of track and football, who was later my coach and adviser at Kentucky State College when I was a student looking for direction.

Not many can say, "I had a teacher or teachers in high school who really inspired me and made all the difference." It's a pivotal time of life. While trying not to show it, you are in fact looking around for guidance. You're a student learning so much that's new, like how to be socialized, how to do algebra, how to speak French, act, write, punt, debate, serve the community, make friends, know love from attraction—all while undergoing huge, rapid changes in mind, character, and body, leaving childhood behind, running the gauntlet of teenage years, and arriving on the doorstep of adulthood. Not many people can say, "But for a word of encouragement from him, a word of guidance from her, my life would have been very different and not half as fulfilling." I am among those who, with love and gratitude, can say these things about my high school teachers.

Mrs. Perry and Mrs. Williams were more than teachers. They were also surrogate parents or aunts. They were women who went above and beyond for their students. They regarded these children as their sacred trusts, and they worked hard to elicit the best from them, getting them to do things they never thought they could do. Their style was kind but in-your-face when things weren't going well and very encouraging when things were. Above all, they were nurturing to kids in need of nurture.

Our high school was, in every way it could be, as all-American as any high school of the era. Its atmosphere was a balance between the formal, in which hard work, attention, and respect were unquestionably expected, yet friendly. The formal came out in the guidepost written to us by our principal, Lonnie Howard Threadgill:

> Today, as youth leaves the world of high school and its joys, it will
> be met by the seriousness of living in an age of unprecedented
> international rivalry and atomic power. On the shoulders of
> youth will be placed the consequences of that power.

The administration and office staff have labored in every way to provide our young people with those intangible qualities that will endow them with solemn dignity and the responsibility of carrying out society's ideals of character, scholarship, leadership, and service.

A slightly different note was struck in a long note to me, written in impeccable Palmer method handwriting by Mrs. Williams:

Dear Ben,

You have proven yourself to be capable and worthy of respect. It has been a privilege to know you and work with you. You are now about to launch forth in a new venture—college and the great, shining future; yes, that future can be shining and can be great as long as you remember that life is good to those who never fail to be true and faithful, to those whose every utmost effort is "to strive, to seek, to find, and not to yield."

It brings tears to my eyes, that last line from Tennyson's "Ulysses." Ulysses is now old, with his travels and sufferings behind him, but after a few years as king back on his home island of Ithaca, he decides to strike out again for adventures new. That is the self-reliant, indomitable attitude Mrs. Williams wants me to adopt. Her praise for me is that I am "capable" and "worthy of respect." A rather sober accolade, true, but coming from her, such words were tremendous, golden gifts. To think Mrs. Williams would see me as having earned them! She also is reminding me of the work and discipline ahead. Encouragement and instruction to the last.

Ours was a small, circumscribed environment, granted. In the society of that era, parents felt justified in correcting or even punishing another family's child if that child got out of line. Much of the time, they were thanked by that child's parents later rather than, as is the case today, being told to mind their own business. That's a distinction between that age and this. As of 2015, if you correct or discipline someone else's child, you're routinely told, "Don't you mess with my child! It's my child, and I'll raise him/her any way I choose to. What rights have you?" That's the point, though: as of the mid-twentieth century, adults assumed they did have the right. Children were a communal project. It could be a rough upbringing, but at least you were getting attention and, in many cases, being saved from your own bad choices in the absence of your parents. This notion that children are the communal responsibility of all adults lay behind the way we were taught and challenged at Broad Street.

I would eventually become a good student and a prominent professional. But at the start, school was a challenge for a little guy who'd grown up on the farm. Socially, it could be a little tough since in school, there was a big difference between the town kids and the country kids. "Farmer" was not a nickname of praise, and it was a nickname I got a lot when someone wanted to get a rise out of me. I got the hang of things, though. I'd seen my older siblings go through the cycle of study and challenge and achievement, and I had watchful eyes shepherding me up every rung.

I can't remember much about grade school or middle school. I wasn't the only farmer's kid learning how to be socialized, and many of my town friends were unruly and rough around the edges. By the time I got to high school, I had study skills, discipline, and a fair degree of academic confidence. I also had siblings and parents poised to let me know about it if I let them down. There was the family honor to uphold, for one thing. My brothers and sisters made it clear to me: "You have to conduct yourself a certain way. You have to make good grades. We want to see your results." They helped me with my studies. I was the youngest, and I was malleable. I wanted to please my brothers and sisters, and I accepted their suggestions.

We were children whose marks and achievements mattered. I liked reading and math. One of my brothers, David, didn't like to study, but he was naturally gifted and didn't have to study much. He could take tests and "magically" earn top marks. My sister Colleen was valedictorian of her class, with excellent grades. She was very intense. If during her homework she encountered a math problem she couldn't do, she would cry over it. She'd go to bed crying if she couldn't figure it out.

Their reputations preceded me into high school. After one history exam, our teacher, Mrs. Martin, brought up my paper and discussed it in front of the class, criticizing the way I had handled the questions, and she said that I had misinterpreted what was required. When she handed back the paper, it had a C+ on it. The fellow in the desk next to me saw that and said, "Man, I thought you'd flunked!" Mrs. Martin was expecting me to stand out as my siblings had stood out. It really did jump-start my determination to do well in history, which was not one of my stronger classes.

Our teachers did things like that to goad us on, to make us work harder or try different things. Debate class with Mrs. Perry and drama class with Mrs. Williams were like this. I guarantee you that few of us ever had imagined we'd get up and speak in public, much less take a role in an actual play and act out a part. Sure, for someone like Morgan Freeman, who was born to act, things came as second nature. Not for me or my friends Charles and Alexander. None of us had ever done such things. In debate class and in the debate club, however, Mrs. Perry insisted on getting us to stand up and reason out difficult subjects under the pressure of public scrutiny. She taught us that throughout history, liberal education was meant to get people ready for civic life. That was how the Greeks and Romans got their youth ready for leadership. Students in Greenwood didn't know that then, of course, but Mrs. Perry did, and so we debated and debated. It taught us much about language, comportment, grace, argument, reasoning, and the psychology of persuasion. These were things that no educated person couldn't afford not to learn.

Likewise, Mrs. Williams got us out on the stage and, against all likelihood, made Charles and me into actors. We had a pretty fine forty-person strong drama club, and we won a state prize in 1955 for outstanding performance. Theater had its own world of things to teach us, like the nature of teamwork and the intricacies of stagecraft involving logistics, timing, interplay, and physical matters, such as blocking and lighting, not to mention the power of elegant, forceful language. These things were more than academic pursuits to our teachers, and they made sure we learned why. Debate and drama were meant to teach us difficult, pressurized endeavors calling for mastery, patience, practice, confidence, attention, and empathy. We had to leave ourselves and assume new roles. We had to enter their worlds and learn to live there.

My friend Charles Smith was a great example of the benefits of such encouragement. In the early days of high school, Charles hung back a little and was not really part of the crowd. But Ms. Williams really worked with him and turned him into a creditable actor, something I know he'd never even thought himself able to do. Mrs. Perry and Mrs. Williams were, in their own ways, shaping our characters and preparing us to be adults.

This is why it's such a shame our educational system devalues arts and humanities. We've forgotten what they are meant to do, and we have ceased to give these studies the chance to do exactly what our teachers made sure they did for us. My friend Alexander Scott quoted *Macbeth* to me in my yearbook, both to recall our many happy hours shared in drama and also to say, "Let's use the lives we've been given . . . Life's but a walking shadow, a poor player that struts and frets his hour upon the stage and then is heard no more. Best wishes, Alexander." My friend Ernye Roberson, a fellow drama devotee, quoted Iago in *Othello*, reminding me that it is "in ourselves that we are thus or thus." They knew. Our teachers knew. We all knew. The school systems of today have forgotten.

My leadership skills began by Mrs. Perry's instigation. She kept encouraging me to run for president of the class and president of the student council. I did then, and I won throughout high school and college. I spent years getting chosen by my peers for leadership positions. Mrs. Perry cultivated a characteristic I didn't know I had.

Throughout high school, I was class president and student council president. The effect of these elections worked in a virtuous circle. Once elected, I tried to live up to the confidence expressed in me by my peers. After the first time, I got elected over and over. Any politician knows it's how it works. It's infectious. My teachers saw leadership in me and encouraged it. My fellow students encouraged it too: "This guy can lead us. He has a certain way of holding himself, a certain character, a dedication." I accepted it and never backed away from it.

I was also chosen to be captain of the football team. I was the quarterback. Coaches Thomas and Leonard saw the leadership qualities also and drove me to accept the position of captain. I wasn't what they now call a jock. I wasn't interested only in sports or even mainly in sports, but I participated.

When I was a kid, my pals and I would play whatever was available, whatever was in season. We'd throw a football around. My daddy played baseball at Philander Smith College. He was a pitcher and, from what I've heard, a very good one, although he was never one to play sports with his kids. He didn't want us to be that athletic; he wanted us to concentrate on our academics. Sometimes Daddy would tell me about the pitches he threw: the inshoot or outshoot, as they used to call them then (what they call cutters and sliders now), or the drop, the fearsome twelve-to-six curveball that sank away just as the batter swung. Daddy never showed me how this was done. He didn't want me to get involved.

I chose football, and my father didn't want me to play that either. During my sophomore year, Coach Leonard came out to the house, and he told Daddy I had skills and could play. Coach must have persuaded Daddy, because a little while later, my father said, "If you want to play football, you can play." Some of this reluctance, I think, was an act. My father was sincere in wanting me to concentrate on academics, which I did. While I might have been captain of the team, I wasn't part of the wider milieu of football, sports, or athletes. Few of my friends were footballers. We played the game together, but after practice or games, I gravitated to people who were more academically inclined. Sports was not a bond. I was never going to be only an athlete. Not ever. I used to hear rumors around town that Daddy would drop into conversation certain remarks about me playing football. People would say, "Your daddy says that you're the best on the team." He would never say that to me directly, but evidently, he took a certain degree of pleasure in telling it to others.

Around April, when the weather was predictable, Coach Leonard would say, "All right, boy, we're going to get you out here every day after school." He would also bring a center, running back, wide receiver together, and for an hour or more, we worked on quarterbacking, a complex and technical position full of nuances and strategy. Real team training started in August, and that was when he started working with me on punting also because he thought I'd have a lot of striking power when I kicked the ball because of my long legs and big feet. When the season started my junior year, I knew the offense very well. I was the starting quarterback on the varsity team my junior year, at a time when juniors were not usually allowed to do that. I was also elected team cocaptain.

*Sports*

Football played a role in cultivating leadership in me transcended to my student council and class president positions. The quarterback is the leader of the team on offense, so it's natural that he's also a leader generally. It's an honor to be elected team captain. It means your teammates have confidence in you.

Sports can build character, confidence, and self-reliance. Sports can't be an end in itself. Sports in school can teach us friendship, teamwork, diligence, patience, achievement, logistics, math and keep us physically fit. What I gained from sports fed directly into what I gained from drama, speech, math, and farmwork. In my yearbook, Coach Thomas drew these connections when he wrote, "As a general on the gridiron, you will be missed at Broad Street High School. I sincerely hope you will carry on the winning tradition wherever you go and in whatever you endeavor to do."

In my senior year, I sat on the bench exactly once when our team was playing another team that was really going to wallop us, and the coach wanted to get a look at another, younger quarterback who'd be leading the team the next year. My replacement didn't do too well, so for the sake of team respect, the coach put me back in.

One night during my junior year, we were playing Bowman High School from Vicksburg, Mississippi. It was a miserable night, and the field was slippery. Without much experience, I was sent in to play defense. I wasn't having too much success as Bowman liked to run a single-wing offense, and they had come down the field and were now in a goal-line stand. We packed in close to stop them from getting the touchdown, and their offensive line got set to throw everything they could at us. The quarterback took the snap; the Bowman line surged forward, and as always happens in goal-line stands, large, heavy bodies fell left and right. I got wedged in, and somebody ran into my knee. I fell awkwardly, in terrible pain.

Mortified, I avoided all eyes as the medics loaded me into the ambulance for the ride to the hospital. Daddy accompanied me back home from the hospital—I was lying in the ambulance—a week later, in a body cast. As the ambulance rolled toward home, jolts of agony riding up my leg with each bump and pothole, Daddy leaned toward me and said, "You get better and you go back out there and play. You show them." I was utterly shocked. Here was my daddy, who hadn't even wanted me to play football, holding me up and telling me to get back out and prove I could do it.

That was a big, big thing in my life. It has stayed with me ever since. *Get back out there and show them you can take it. Don't walk away, not from this, not from anything.* I have applied it to everything in my adult life, to the difficulties of college, to my practice, to everything. I have had many opportunities to reflect on what my daddy did for me that night. He was telling me he had confidence that I could and would heal and excel.

I had a badly broken left leg and a fractured kneecap. These would take months to heal and years to get all the way better. Daddy supported and strengthened his lesson to me. He told me, "You will get better and play again and show them." I had to lie on my back for three months and couldn't turn over. Daddy was by my side and taught me how to endure, focus, and heal. Everything, even discomfort, is a means to an end. Work toward that end.

I did return for my senior year. I worked hard to regain strength and flexibility, and I played the whole season. I would not really regain 100 percent mobility in my leg until my third year in college. In the meantime, I learned as much as I could about how to play the game. My skills improved, and I would never again get seriously hurt. Coaches Leonard and Thomas helped me also. They ordered a special brace to protect my leg and converted an offensive lineman to play fullback and block for me. Coming back from a badly broken leg meant I had to work that much harder and improve quickly. I accomplished both.

In school, I had the duties of student council, which included my pal Charles Blackmon as business manager and pal Alexander Scott as assistant business manager. I was statistician for the basketball team, which indulged my taste for math. I was also in the Hi-Y club, directed by Coach Leonard. The Hi-Y clubs, very popular at the time, were the YMCA's program for the high schools. The program's stated purpose was to "create, maintain and extend to the fullest capacity of one's ability, throughout the home, school and community, high standards of moral character through improvement, brother/sisterhood, equality, and service in High Schools." Both the Hi-Y and its female counterpart, the Tri-Hi-Y club, were huge in Greenwood, and meetings and projects were well attended. Public service could include anything from cleaning parks, visiting the sick, or distributing blankets, clothes, and food to the less fortunate. Hi-Y had manuals and pins for membership and achievement and a code of behavior. The program was yet another way to encourage students to keep the bar high in their spiritual, public, and personal lives.

My friend Charles Blackmon was always there. If my attention wandered or if I went off and did something dumb, he'd be sure to get me back straight in line. I did the same for him, but he was a good man and didn't need much straightening. It's interesting to note how Charles came in line with the village of people around me, which consisted of my parents, siblings, teachers, and coaches, in the big project of moving me forward.

Students during that time in Greenwood did that for one another. We were helping form one another's character without even knowing it. I cannot think of a better definition of *friendship*. My friend and fellow student Alma Greene wrote this to me in my yearbook, sounding the theme so often sounded at Broad Street from friend to friend, student to student: "I watched you grow up, and I can certainly say I am proud of the man you turned out to be." We had our eyes on one another and took it seriously. It seems to me, our obligation was to do as well as we could and encourage one another to do the same.

I should mention that by the time I got to high school, our family's circumstances had changed. We had an actual car. A big rackety truck came into our lives when I was in eighth grade. My sister Mary Jean learned how to drive, and from then on, we often drove to school or much of the way at least. What we actually did was park the truck at the house of a cousin who lived somewhat closer to school. Our cousins would keep an eye on the truck, and we walked the rest of the way there, picking up the truck on the way back. While I'm sure that daily three-mile walk to and from school had built character for my first eight years of schooling, I can tell you we did welcome the ride.

I was fortunate. No one I knew was rich. No one I knew was privileged. I had known a youth of very hard physical labor and equally hard intellectual endeavor. We were black, remember, in Mississippi, graduating just before the start of the civil rights movement. With all the odds against us, we had youthful joys and enjoyed being in high school and doing high school things. My pal Charles, now that our ways would part after high school, wrote wistfully, "It was a pleasant life while we were together as pals. . . . Watch yourselves in the clinches and break clean. See you in that glorious ending."

We managed to have pretty wonderful lives, but all, even our fondest moments in high school, were set against these facts. It's amazing we survived it all.

# CHAPTER 3

# THE WAY IT WAS: RACE RELATIONS AND MY FAMILY

I cannot say enough in praise of my parents and teachers in getting us ready for the rest of our lives. My wonder and gratitude increase when I consider where and when I grew up. Mississippi at that time was the lynchingest state in the Union, fertile ground for each successive wave of the Ku Klux Klan and for the white supremacist and ultraviolent reactionary groups that arose in the 1950s to oppose integration of schools, workplaces, and society. I grew up in that decade, going from grade school to high school and to college. When I look back, I am amazed not only that I made it, thanks to my family and teachers, but also that I achieved what I did. It reminds me that I did nothing alone and was armed with the careful love of those around me. Credit the village.

Almost nobody who wrote in my high school yearbook in 1956 mentioned race. You can take that in a couple of different directions. Our teachers were focused on encouraging us for our future lives. No one said, "Well, good luck, but you know that whites and blacks don't get along" or "Try hard but don't expect much—the deck is stacked against anyone with dark skin." They were going to congratulate us and showed us love and care before letting us go. Their fond farewells were like those from any caring faculty to any bright, promising group of young people about to step off into adulthood.

But there's another way to see this surprising silence among the faculty and students of an all-black school in the racially torn state of Mississippi, late 1950s. "The way it was" was so obvious, so pervasive, and such a fact of life that it went without mention. It would be like mentioning air, food, or sunlight. Danger, furthermore, attached to the mere mention of *racial animus* or *mistreatment by whites*. Nobody was going to commit such thoughts to writing; even if those thoughts were in our minds, very few—almost nobody—would even say such things, as obvious and pervasive as they were everywhere around us.

I want to look at "the way it was," how it expressed itself in our lives and how we handled it when it stood in our way or menaced us. I was a levelheaded, circumspect child. As the last "surprise" baby in the family, I was raised by everyone around me with love and daily life lessons. And really, that's the point of this whole book. Those lessons helped me avoid the dangers facing a young black man in Mississippi at that time. That upbringing taught me how to get along with people, no matter their color. Such skills helped me become a leader in high school and on the football teams I quarterbacked. They helped me persevere when my way was blocked, difficult, or unclear. I believe they made me a good dentist and a good professional.

## I Thought of Emmett Till

Money, Mississippi, the town in which Emmett Till was lynched and murdered, was 10.9 miles from Greenwood. Till, a boy from Chicago, was visiting family in Money and was murdered on August 28, 1955, the summer of my junior year. Till was fourteen; he is said to have approached, whistled, or spoken to Carolyn Bryant, a young woman who ran a grocery store in Money. Till was soon dead, in gruesome fashion, which included beating, torture, mutilation, and a bullet to the head. After his body was found well downstream in the Tallahatchie River, two men, Roy Bryant, husband of Carolyn, and his half-brother, J. W. Milam, were tried for the murder.

The trial was held in Sumner, 38.1 miles from my home. It is astonishing and heartbreaking, looking back, to realize how shamefully brief the trial was, even with the national furor over the murder. Feelings were stoked in part by the open casket at Till's memorial service, revealing the corpse's nauseatingly disfigured head and face.

The jury was all white. Tallahatchie County sheriff Clarence Strider was heard to greet black spectators entering the courthouse by saying, "Hello, niggers." On the fifth day, the jury deliberated sixty-seven minutes before acquitting the two defendants. One juror was quoted as saying, "If we hadn't stopped to drink pop, it wouldn't have taken that long."

Despite these infamous events, the proceedings had seen moments of great heroism.

Mose Wright, Till's great-uncle, then sixty-four, was a farmer and minister with a two-bedroom cabin in Money. Till was staying at his house on the night of the murder. The murderers came to the house and bullied Wright into telling them whether Till was there. At the trial, the defense argued it had been too dark for Wright to identify Bryant and Milam with any certainty. The lawyers clearly thought a black man would be too scared to stand up in a public court and finger a white man for murdering another black man. But Wright did—and photographs exist to prove it. Wright, visibly terrified, collapsed into his chair afterward, emotionally drained. He also endured a furious half-hour cross-examination by defense attorney Sidney Canton. During that badgering, as many witnesses noticed, Wright stopped saying the obligatory "sir" expected from all black men when they addressed white men.

Wright's performance, as many noted at that time, was a small but clear indication that things were changing in America. The almost-gleeful racism at the trial, the open manner in which the murderers boasted to others about the killing, even showing Till's body in the back of a truck to other people, suggests how far above the law some white people felt when it came to mistreating blacks. As I write today, I can say that while many injustices still afflict black people, many unrighteous inequalities, it will be hard for a murder like that of Emmett Till to happen today and much harder for a trial like that to occur without consequence.

The almost unbelievably savage killing galvanized the black community. On December 1, 1955, little more than two months after that disgraceful verdict, the Montgomery, Alabama, bus boycott began, touching off the modern civil rights era in the United States. Rosa Parks, the pioneering central figure in those boycotts, refused a bus driver's order to go to the back of the bus, the section reserved for blacks. She later said that at that moment, when she stayed put in her seat, "[she] thought of Emmett Till, and [she] just couldn't go back."

It's an infamous trial and a notorious, hideous crime. I wouldn't have rehearsed the facts above except to begin a discussion about "the way it was" when and where I grew up. We lived upright and cautious lives in the midst of social circumstances in which we were regarded as zeroes. All of us were working hard toward the future, with a sober eye on the present. That makes it even more surprising to consider how well so many of us, family and schoolmates alike, ended up doing. Racism, of an ignorant, murderous, insistent, indomitable kind, was the single most obvious and important social dynamic flowing around us. Yet despite what was facing us, we found ways to have lives, nurture our characters, and construct our futures. I hope it's of use to my readers to reflect, amid our continuing racial troubles, on how we managed to do this.

The impact of the Emmett Till murder was not noticeable. I asked people much later, "Do you remember how you felt when all this was going on?" And they didn't. I don't remember my parents saying anything about it.

This might seem confusing on the surface of it. How could a murder that galvanized the civil rights movement, a murder that made the papers on both coasts, not make more of an impact? Remember one thing: a lot of people probably did have deep feelings at that time, from disgust to sorrow to rage, but did not dare express them. You just didn't. No one wants trouble, and few of us go looking for it. Had you spoken out, or let it be known you even had an opinion, you could well lose your job and, perhaps, your life. It is easy, often a necessity for survival, to get into the habit of letting well enough alone. Many people, no matter what they may have felt back then, are content to do just that, in memory and testimony.

Mississippi had a rich history of lynching. It was not unusual. Records at the Tuskegee Institute at Tuskegee University in Alabama suggest that between 1882 and 1968, there were 591 lynchings in Mississippi; all but forty-two of them were lynchings of black people. That's more than in any other state, more lynchings and more blacks killed.

If you were black, Mississippi literally was the most dangerous place in America to live in. Our parents taught us how to comport ourselves, show respect, still our anger, check our reactions, and let trouble pass us by. They did not raise us to be passive—remember, their strategy lay in education, in getting us to excel via our minds and our merits. They worked to get us into a different future. The goal was to have a good life, away from the soil, away from Mississippi, away from "the way it was."

It was not unusual to hear of someone getting killed. By the same token, such deaths did not attract much discussion. Had Emmett Till been a boy from Mississippi and not a boy from Chicago on a fatal visit, his death might not even have been much remarked. But he was from Chicago, and so was his mother, Mamie Till Bradley. Had she lived in Mississippi, it would have been more than likely she would have worked for a white boss in some position or a black boss who worked for a white boss. Unless she had been very heroic and singular, the facts on the ground would have ensured her silence. But Mamie Till Bradley was from Chicago and didn't have those restrictions. She made sure his death got into the national media. Her decision to show her son's bloated, mutilated corpse at his memorial service was both brutal and brilliant: it forced awareness into millions of minds. Had she not taken that almost-unimaginable step, I wonder how much ink Emmett Till's death would ever have gotten. Yet that was exactly the type of extreme measure the situation called for.

At school, as I remember, there were times when somebody would not be seen at school for a while, simply stopping coming. After a while, we'd start missing that person. We never learned but always wondered what happened to him or her. We were taught by family and friends alike not to probe too far into the matter. This was hardly an everyday thing, but it was not rare either. These were the deaths and disappearances that would never appear on any ledger, in any statistic. Many bodies would never be found. Such disappearances just happened, and there would be no explanation. No one would say anything, and no one would ask. As I look back, I can say we knew these were the kinds of things that could happen to you. If you did something they did not like, people could hang you from a tree, beat you to death, shoot you, or throw you in a river. We learned early not to inquire, not to say anything, if you knew what was good for you.

It seems scarier to me now than it seemed at that time. It was just the way it was. I often think about what could have happened if the players in the Till story were one of my friends or playmates, like Nell Connerly or one of the Bufords. What happened to Emmett Till was unbelievably horrible, but it was the extremity of an all-too-familiar, established truth. That was the way many white men felt about their women: white women could be considered dishonored were they so much as addressed by a black man. A white baby was angelic; a black baby was nothing. Contact with black people was polluting.

It could lead to complex sexual politics. As my daddy told me, "Son, you're going to realize that two of the freest people in the world are the white man and the black woman. They can do anything they want to do and get away with it. A white man and a black woman can have a relationship without getting into trouble about it, but if it's a white woman and a black man, somebody's going to die." He was doing more than giving me a fatherly lecture on sexual mores. He was pointing out that the black man had severe limitations on him, violation of which could lead to his death. In the same way, the white woman was hedged in by severe codes of probity, honor, and purity. The two could not mix, could not even meet. The white man, of course, was the alpha, the free dominant.

The black woman, as I mentioned previously, was an interesting case. Many black women could find work more easily than black men could. They were seen as unthreatening and unpolluted. Black women worked in white households and raised many of the white families of the South at that time as surrogate teachers and mothers. As you recall, my mother arose from such a white household, from such a white-and-black union. The white man's freedom and the black woman's relative, unthreatening mobility and relatively cheap and available labor made it possible—and in a strange way, even safe, relatively speaking—for such relations to exist. This was just another lesson in our continuing life-class about race.

## Our Neighbors

One time, and this is a very clear memory, talkative Mr. George Buford, the grandfather of one of the neighboring white families, came over, as he often did, to chew the fat with Daddy. I can just see him now walking down the road with his walking cane and his full head of white hair. They were seated on the porch when talk turned to a not-uncommon theme.

"Mr. Buford, do you really believe things will ever be that way in this country?" my daddy asked. "That black and white will really live together? That the difference in color won't matter anymore and a person will just be a person?" He asked this with some incredulity.

Mr. George Buford said, "I really do. Maybe not in our lifetimes or our children's lifetimes, though, I'd like to think that. But it's coming. It's going to be. I know! I study human nature!"

I recall being impressed with two things: that the two men—one white, one black—could talk relaxed and calm like that about a subject like that, in an unheated exchange of views, without bad feelings of any kind, and that of the two of them, it was the white man who expressed not just willingness for "that day" to come but also hope and belief that it would, which tells you that even as a little boy, I sometimes wondered about that very thing myself.

The fact that we had white neighbors on either side of us and also parents who insisted on respect and fairness and who showed that respect and fairness in all their dealings with the said neighbors had a good impact on all of us children. We felt less-overt racial tension than some other black people did because, comparatively, we lived in a white environment. We saw the Bufords and the Connerlys all the time, and we got along with them. That gave me something I've taken through life: easiness with all people. It's not just tolerance. I think it goes beyond that. It's an ability, taught by parents, teachers, siblings, and classmates, to see everybody as people, to see them as deserving all the good things I hope for myself. I'm not saying I'm a great person, but I know what I was taught, I did try to live that way, and it really helped me through life.

My next-door neighbor Glen was a year younger than me, and his daddy was a cow trader. Sometimes Glen would ask if I could go with them when his daddy went to cattle auctions, and he'd say, "Yeah, Ben can go." We'd all go out there. We were five, six, seven, and eight years old, and while the trading was going on, we were running around the auction place. I remember one man asked Glen's daddy, Brooks, "Brooks, are both these kids yours?" He'd laugh and say, "Yeah, damn, both of them are mine." And I went home and told my parents, who had a laugh over that. But Glen's daddy had his eye out for me. If somebody had tried to bother me, I truly believe he would have ripped them apart.

To show you how relaxed the relations among the various children were, I can tell you about Nell Connerly, a daughter of one of the white families. Nell used to come over a lot, and we'd play together, or she'd come around just to hang out and talk, sometimes while I was doing chores. She was a little older than me, and we got to be good friends. She'd come over in her Daisy Dukes and just watch me work. No supervision. No one worried about it. Nell was pretty, but I never got any ideas, because you just didn't in those days. I think back on those times and wonder what would have happened if, say, a white man had lost his dog and came looking for it on our property, and he came upon this pretty young white girl and younger black boy together. All sorts of things could have happened. I guess the point is that they didn't. These were neighbors and playmates. As a matter of course, white and black children might play together as rough and virtual equals while they were little, but once the white children got to be fifteen or sixteen, it was expected that black children would address them as, say, "Mr. George" or "Ms. Nell." But around our houses, we never did that. It was a different matter if we ever saw them in a public situation, like on the streets in town. Very different.

Always implicit and in the background, you had the fact of race and the ancient and unshakable facts. Mother and Daddy showed the white families unflagging respect and neighborliness and helped each family out on numerous occasions, as good neighbors would. And as you've seen, Mother was very good at running interference when one white family was at odds with the other. But by the same token, all that time, everyone on all sides was observing the rules. There were things you did and things that were not done, and in a way, everyone had to keep his or her eye on those boundaries.

Once or twice, we came that close to catastrophe.

It was a rainy day, and when it rained, you couldn't do much work on a farm. Actually, I liked it when it rained; it meant I could take a nap. So I, then six or seven, was fast asleep as the drama unfolded. Unfold it did. Colleen and Mary Jean and two of the Buford girls, Margie and Ina Jean, were playing at our house and got into a raging argument. I was little then, and I can't recall what started it or even what it was about. The Buford girls ran home and told Mrs. Buford, and the sense of insult escalated, getting worse each time the story was retold. When Mr. Brooks Buford got home, his wife told him, and he went nearly out of his mind.

Mr. Buford stomped down the road a quarter mile, fuming all the way and getting angrier and angrier. When he got to our house, he started yelling, irate and threatening.

"You want to live here by me? You want to live here by me?" he kept shouting, which was pretty ironic, since the Bufords lived on land once owned by my grandfather. But as he stood there yelling, half-crazy, Mr. Buford knew that in a conflict, he as a white man would have the upper hand.

On and on he went. "This happened and that happened, and my girls said your girls did this and said that."

Thank goodness Daddy was not at home! Mother took the lead and went out into the yard and tried to calm Mr. Buford down. He respected her: as the two talked, his voice lowered, his entire aspect relaxing. At last he left.

I was deep asleep when I was startled awake—somebody was gently waking me up. I shook off the sleep and opened my eyes, and there was Mr. Brooks Buford.

I was all confused, but what had happened was, some time had passed, Mr. Buford had walked home, and then he had a change of heart and came back.

"Ben," he said, "I'm sorry. I came down here, like you saw, and I've been a fool. I cussed and carried on. I talked to your good mother, though, and she calmed me down. That woman up there"—he gestured down the road, referring to Mrs. Buford—"she's going to get me in trouble. I love all you people. Ben, will you forgive me?"

"Yes, I will." What else was I going to say?

Mr. Buford went to my mother and Colleen and Mary Jean personally and asked for their forgiveness. Then he went home. My mother went to each one of us right after that and said, "Not a word to your daddy about what happened here this afternoon. Not a word." And we had the good sense never to tell him. Daddy died without ever hearing a word of it.

One other thing about that day we never told him. My brother Clyde, ten years older than me, the one who later became an educator and tax assessor in Greenwood, saw Mr. Buford come down the road and head straight for our house. He saw Mother go out into the yard to try to defuse the man's fury. And he saw Mr. Buford advance on our mother.

That was all he needed to see. He went, and he found Daddy's pistol (guns were something the farmer needed), checked that it was loaded, and went out to the porch as Mother tried to talk Mr. Buford down. Now, the eaves of our porch roof came down pretty low, so Clyde held the pistol up over his head, under the eaves, so no one could see he was holding a gun.

After Mr. Buford left, Mary Jean asked Clyde, "What were you doing with Daddy's pistol?"

And he answered, "If he hit my mother, I was going to kill him."

And he would have, he would have.


## Uncle Floyd

While all black folks knew very well what was going on, not all black folks agreed on how you should feel about it—or at least how you should express yourself about it. The safest way, as I've discussed, was to keep your feelings to yourself, show nothing, go along to get along. This was the wisdom our parents taught us: the way blacks were treated was wrong, was against the law of God and the law of the Constitution. But it made no sense to be a martyr about it. Our best strike against the system was to do well for ourselves, to get to such a point of achievement that there would be nothing anyone could say to or against us.

Uncle Floyd Key lived and farmed on our land for several years. We called a corner of our property Uncle Floyd's Land because Daddy and Mother had brought him on with ten to fifteen acres of his own on which to farm cotton. To be sure, Uncle Floyd worked hard because he had to, as we all did. And as you might expect, at harvesttime, he'd come help my parents, and they would help him get everything done and all the crops brought in.

I didn't know Uncle Floyd too well, but from what I heard, he was different. He was an angry man in a way my daddy wasn't. The racial situation in this country had brought out bitterness in Uncle Floyd, a frustration and dissatisfaction with his lot. My parents, of course, knew what all that was about, but bitterness wasn't their way, and they taught us not to share it. Besides, I suspect Daddy did not think Floyd was much of a farmer, disposed maybe to complain too much and not doing enough to improve his land or his lot. Floyd was also a bit of a ladies' man and constantly went to Greenwood in search of companionship. My upright Methodist father wasn't too much a fan of that either. Eventually, Uncle Floyd gave up farming, and along with an entire generation of African Americans in the South, he "broke north," going up to Chicago to make a living.

## Racism, Conscious and Unconscious: The Trickle-Down Effect

You had to put up with certain things. There were ritual humiliations and underhanded spite in race relations of the day, and you'd be truly foolish to question or fight them.

We had white men who would come on to our property and hunt birds. My daddy sometimes had to post a No Trespassing sign to try to discourage people from abusing his property like that, but for white landowners and their friends, such signs meant nothing. Riding their elegant horses, they would simply ride right on to our property with their bird dogs and guns, and there was nothing Daddy could do about it. He knew that if he went out and tried to dissuade them, the result would not be pleasant. They could do what they wanted to do on your land. They often had a single black man riding with them, perhaps on an broken-down old mule. This black man would have a sack, and it was his job to jump off his mule when the white men downed a bird and stuff it in that sack for them, and later, he'd also clean and prepare it.

This was the kind of thing you saw as a kid. The white men simply assumed, correctly, that they could ride onto a black man's property with impunity and hunt to their hearts' content. The disdain and condescension were overwhelming. But that was the way life was then. I can look back at it now and say, "How unfair that was." But that was the way it was, the way life was, and you accepted it for what it was. Above all, you said nothing to anybody.

I had a white friend named Bobby Avant who was an athlete at Greenwood High, the white high school, just as I was at mine. Our schools never faced each other, but away from town and to ourselves, Bobby and I often practiced together in my pasture, throwing and catching the ball, practicing routes, that kind of thing. If I saw Bobby in town the next day, walking down the street, he might not even acknowledge me, or if he did, it would be the merest of acknowledgments. If he were with friends, he would never tell them, "That's Ben Nero. He plays quarterback for Broad Street High School, and he throws a nice, sharp spiral." Most likely, he wouldn't say anything. My white female friends would never have spoken to me at all.

## Race at School

"The way things were" percolated into our high school life. Mr. William Barnett Dribben was the superintendent of the Greenwood School District when I was in high school. The district encompassed both white and black schools, but they were kept strictly separate, in academics, in sports, in everything.

We didn't see Mr. Dribben very often at Broad Street School. He visited our school two or three times a year. He was always at Greenwood High School, the white high school, and he pretty much stayed there whenever he came to town. That was always the way it was. You just pretty much knew. You didn't complain about it. It was just the way it was.

Now, I have no question that Mr. Dribben was completely dedicated in his own mind and career to the cause of education. He was in education his whole life, becoming superintendent of the Greenwood district and also for those of Benoit and Lexington. He would retire in 1974 and pass away in 2002. When he did visit, however, a certain tone obtained. One day, soon after my broken leg had healed enough for me to return to school, I was working my way down the hall on crutches when I saw Mr. Dribben coming down the hall toward me.

All he said to me was, with a big grin, "What happened to you, boy? You got caught in a bear trap?" That was all he had to say. Here's what that tells you: he never came to our games. He never knew that I was starting quarterback and captain of the team, much less student body president, that I had sustained a badly broken leg, that I had been in the hospital, that recovery had been arduous, and that I had been recuperating for quite some time. His greeting to me felt kind of funny. I may be a little sensitive on this point. I've already told you what a blow that injury was and how much my daddy's support and encouragement meant to me. My very presence in the hall, the fact I was working hard to do well in school, get back on the playing field, have a senior year that would help propel me into the next stage of my life, college, fulfilling my parents' hopes and expectations and those of my teachers, siblings, and classmates—all this was very emotional, tied up in working hard side by side with my family and trying to have a future different from my present.

I wonder whether, had I been white, attending Greenwood High School instead of Broad Street High, Mr. Dribben would at least have heard of me and my story. Whether, seeing me coming back from such a grievous injury, he might not have shown some understanding and compassion. I didn't think of myself as some celebrity, and I never expected adults to make much of me. But it was not only a hurtful, inconsiderate comment; it also showed how little engaged Mr. Dribben was with Broad Street.

Sports were big at the high schools, as it usually is at most high schools. Our football, basketball, and track teams belonged to the all-black Big Eight conference, four high schools in the north of the state and four in the south. We were very often division champs in our conference, and often, we were state champs. But you see, we never got any recognition from the white population in Greenwood. The folks at Greenwood High didn't go to our games, and of course, we didn't go to theirs. We weren't allowed to sit in their bleachers. I guess if we'd gone over there, we could have stood behind the end zone, but that never happened. We always wanted to play those guys so we could beat up on them pretty good, but that was never going to happen either.

I am calling no one a racist. I am documenting a climate of more or less unconscious disregard and privilege. You could see this in Mr. Dribben's relationship with our school's principal, Mr. Threadgill. He had written in our yearbooks a bracing call for responsibility in an age of changing social relations and nuclear anxiety. Mr. Threadgill, a Knoxville College man, was a conscientious and hardworking teacher and school administrator who would have a long career in Greenwood schools. By the time he was finished, he'd have a high school in Greenwood named after him in recognition of his legacy.

Mr. Threadgill was a micromanager. He wanted us to be always on the ball. He kept after the teachers to work hard and get us to work hard. When Mr. Dribben came around, you could tell, because Mr. Threadgill would go into overdrive. He'd be here, there, and everywhere, directing people, managing everything very conspicuously to impress this man. When the superintendent visited the school and addressed him, he called him Threadgill, and Mr. Threadgill had to call him Mr. Dribben. And let's say Mr. Dribben gave us a talk in a school assembly, addressing all of us. If he referred to our principal, he referred to him, in front of us, as just Threadgill. You might think high school kids wouldn't notice it, that we'd just let it pass. We noticed it, all right, and we knew what it meant. It was a nuanced but unmistakable ritual humiliation of a man trying to do a good job. It was a way of cutting him down to size in front of the whole school. Worst of all, it was meant to pass unremarked. And it did. That was just the way it was. But when I look back on it now, it showed such disrespect for this man, such disregard for what he'd gone through and was trying to do for us, and I think Mr. Threadgill did a good job.

Racism has a way of trickling down even into the way black people treat one another. It may be unconscious imitation of whites, or it may be overcompensation, trying to show white people you can be as socially upstanding and uphold just as high standards as you think white people expect.

Consider the way people raise their children. Remember how I said that "white babies were angelic" but "black babies were nothing"? Well, it was clear in and around Greenwood that most white people believed that, and the shame was that some black people treated their children as if they did too, thereby unconsciously communicating this terrible untruth to their children. Sometimes you would see black mothers or caretakers treating children that way if white children or white adults were around. If a black child was acting up, as all children will do sometimes, a black mother or nanny would slap that child or strike it or yell. They felt the eyes of the whites upon them, the pressure, the unspoken insult. *You cannot even raise your own children.*

Sometimes, I know, these women would apologize later to their children. They might say to their child, "We didn't mean that. That's just the way things are." But what they were doing was being subservient to the white children or adults around them and letting the white children know that white children were better than their own children. In effect, they were telling their children that they were less, that they were nothing. And this rough, angry way of raising children and the terrible lie it told thus got passed down from generation to generation.

I never had that happen to me with my parents, but I'd seen it. Little black children had to live with this question: Why am I less? The answer was, "Your skin is black, and the others' is white."

## Race and My Family

My family was not to remain untouched by these toxic double and triple standards. I personally was cautious enough never to get into trouble about it. Once again, I was probably protected by my position as the youngest kid: I watched my elders and kept quiet and studied my lessons in school and in life. I was no angel at all, but another thing I usually wasn't was a fool.

I came close. One night during my high school years, I somehow persuaded Daddy to lend me our rattletrap old truck for the evening. Let me tell you, this was not a usual thing. My good friend Charles Blackmon and I, however, wanted to take a road trip. There was a basketball game or something up in Clarksdale, with the possibility of meeting some of the girls afterward. A set of wheels, no matter how shaky, would increase our worth in the eyes of those girls. I don't remember exactly what I told Daddy to get him to lend me the truck, but he lent it to me. So Charles and I went on our evening visit to this town. And I can say that we had a wild night, but not the kind we intended. It got late and it got dark, and it got time to go home. So we started out. With the fatal timing often seen in complex machinery, the truck waited until we were in the middle of nowhere before it died on us. It rolled to a stop beside a country road in pitch-black. This situation was not good. It could even be life-threatening. It was dangerous even to be associated with the truck since many people would assume two young black men were joyriding in a stolen vehicle.

We couldn't stay in the truck, and we couldn't stay where we were. Very few people had telephones, least of all black people. Charles's parents did have one, but mine did not, and at any rate, no one would let two unknown black boys use their phones so late at night. We knew too well even to ask. We had no way, then, to notify our parents, who, the moment we were late, would start fearing the worst. That was the way it was. If your son or daughter was late or turned up missing, your mind went to the most likely explanation. Such nights of terror and agony came to thousands of black parents in those days, and that whole story would never be written. I am only sorry that on this night, I caused my parents that kind of suffering.

Charles and I began to hitchhike into town along Highway 49, dangerous and risky, with many drivers just as ready to shoot you as to pick you up. But an old white man in a big truck did pick us up and drove us to Greenwood. We went to the home of our English and drama teacher, Mrs. Williams, who let us borrow her car along with a rope, with which we towed the truck to a repair place. We got back to town at about 5:00 a.m., where yet another surreal adventure awaited us.

We were about to return the car when, as we drove along, we saw, of all people on Earth, Charles's grandfather wandering in the road with a walking stick. He was an elderly man with mental problems, and Charles said to me, "He shouldn't be out. I'd better talk to him and get him to come home with me. He doesn't know where he is. Will you help me get him in the car?"

His grandfather responded by yelling and beating us with his walking stick. He didn't recognize us and thought we were attackers or robbers. He raised a perfect ruckus. Woken out of bed, one of the people along the street called the police, who arrived just as we were giving up and getting back in the car. This was really bad. You just did not want to be involved, at any time, for any reason, with the police. As we've seen in recent US history with the events in Ferguson, Missouri, and elsewhere, the diseased relationship between law enforcement and people of color is still a big problem. I can tell you, in the mid-1950s, it was more than a problem; it was an established and sometimes-lethal institution. For the second time that night, Charles and I were mortally afraid.

These policemen, to give them their due, were sensible men. They saw Charles's grandfather, tried to speak with him, and saw he wasn't right. We had the police call Charles's grandmother, who answered the phone and vouched for us. We were able to return the car and get both Charles's grandfather and Charles back to his house. I hit the road and walked the familiar three miles out into the country to my house. I didn't get back until seven in the morning.

Sure enough, Mother and Daddy were there waiting. They'd been up all night, grieving and uncertain, scared to death, wondering what had become of me. Thoughts that they might never see me again had probably crossed their minds all the long night. It makes me shiver when I think about what they went through. That was the closest I came. And that was close enough, thanks very much. My brother David, however, would be affected much more seriously.

## David

You've already met my brother David. He was named after my daddy. Everyone else called him brother, but I called him Bobo, a name that stuck because it was hard for little me to say "Brother." He was fifteen years older than I was, the pride and joy of my daddy's life. He was a good student, handsome, gifted with quick perception and articulateness, and he was a good athlete too. I have only very faint memories of him living in the house with the rest of us. That's because of something that happened to David: he left our house suddenly at the age of fifteen, when I was only two.

At that young age, I had no understanding of why he had left or where he was going. I was a little boy, and as I grew up, I knew David lived somewhere else for some foggy reason. But I didn't put much stake in it because it was, again, not uncommon for young boys simply to leave friends, family, home, and school without much explanation. I have only very obscure, remote memories of when he left, and no one talked later about why he had gone.

Much later, when I'd grown up a little and was more curious about such things, I asked Mother and Daddy why David didn't live with us, and they rehashed the whole story. Generally, people tended to let things alone and not bring them up once they were done. David was accused of trying to kiss a white woman—I never learned who—in Greenwood.

Even now as I write this, I just don't believe it happened. My brother David was a talented man of energy and high spirits, but he wasn't crazy, which he would have had to be to do such a thing in the Greenwood, Mississippi, of 1939 or 1940. Such a thing would throw us all into Emmett Till territory. A mere accusation could be enough to take away your job and even your life. As my daddy had taught me, "If the woman is white and the man is black, somebody's going to die."

One of my daddy's white friends came to the farmhouse to find Daddy. "There's a rumor going around in town," he told him, "that your David made an advance to a white woman. And there is talk about them coming out here to get him. I would advise you to get David out of town immediately."

There was little time to argue the matter. My parents were beside themselves with grief and fear for David, so preparations began in haste. David cried, and he tried to explain to them that this situation was like that of Joseph and Potiphar's wife in Genesis. Lest it seems unlikely that a fifteen-year-old would have that reference right at his fingertips, recall that we were a Bible-reading family. True, we didn't make church every Sunday, partly because of the farm and the distance into town, but my parents read the Bible aloud to us frequently; it was one of the few options we had for family entertainment. So we knew the Bible pretty well. Plus, as you can imagine, the story of Joseph, son of an enslaved class who is menaced by the sexual approaches of a woman from the empowered classes of Egypt, spoke clearly to us in our situation.

In Genesis 39:1–20, Joseph is bought as a slave by the Egyptian Potiphar, chief officer of the palace guard for the pharaoh. Potiphar's wife (nameless in Genesis, though later traditions named her Zuleika) tries to seduce Joseph, who resists her advances, enraging her. As Joseph repels her attempts to seduce him into her bed, she grabs him by the coat: "And it came to pass about this time that Joseph went into the house to do his business; and there was none of the men of the house there within. And she caught him by his garment, saying, 'Lie with me.' And he left his garment in her hand, and fled, and got him out."

As you can see, it makes sense for the story of Potiphar's wife to leap into David's head as a parallel to his own situation. My brother had tried to stay away from the white woman, but she was extremely attracted to him. He had tried to get away, but the woman had embraced him against his will. That hug was the problem, and David's resistance to it. Like Potiphar's wife, the white woman was angry at being spurned and was punishing David as Potiphar's wife punished Joseph by telling others that Joseph had accosted her.

Joseph is thrown into prison, and the only thing that saves him from certain death is his miraculous ability to interpret dreams, by which he comes to the notice of the pharaoh, and eventually becomes a lord high overseer in the pharaoh's court. But no such chance awaited our David. His word would never have held up against a white woman's, not in court and not in the white community. If men had visited our house, they would not have listened. Nor would the court system have been on our family's side, assuming the matter even made it to court at all.

Tearfully, our parents packed David's bags. They contacted cousins who lived in Washington, DC, and arranged with them for David to go live there. A one-way bus ticket was purchased, and in the middle of the night, David was put on a bus to leave our house pretty much forever. Bobo, my brother, never returned to Greenwood for any length of time. In fact, he all but never showed his face there until he was drafted into the US Army in World War II. He returned as an accomplished soldier, with such poise and confidence that it turned heads all over town. No one knew why such a cultured, decorated, and mysterious young man would be in our little town. That was the only reason no one raised a fuss at this return to Greenwood: they didn't connect this accomplished military man with the teenager who'd had to take a midnight bus out of town to escape almost-certain death.

To this day, I wish I'd had the benefit of having my older brother David around with the rest of us for a few more years. This was a man who distinguished himself repeatedly in the military and, later, in business, finding success wherever he went. He was also a man whose successful career was, in the end, hobbled by shady business practices that might well have been racially motivated.

I might have been only two when David left, but he and I had a wonderful relationship for the rest of our lives. He'd call now and then and ask about my grades, playing the role of big brother. It got to be that I was more concerned with pleasing my big brother even than pleasing our parents. If ever I admitted to him that I'd gotten lower than an A on something, he'd tell me, Nero-like, how disappointed he was in me, and I worked feverishly until I'd get my grade back up so that David would be proud of me again. He showed pride continually in my progress through high school and later in college and advanced study. He even showed up to watch one of my high school football games.

David was excited when I was accepted into dental school. When I graduated and told him that I was going back for more advanced training, he said to me, "Let me ask you something. You mean to tell me you can go out now and hang up your shingle, practice dentistry, and earn money, but you're going back to school?" I told him yes, and David said, "Boy, there's something wrong with you!" Every time I think of that story, I laugh. In a way, he was expressing delighted admiration and pride that I'd gotten where I'd gotten. Once I completed the extra training, I enrolled for yet another three years for specialization training, and I expected another jest from my big brother. But at that point, he just said, "I have nothing to say. Whatever you do, I'm proud of you." That was how our family worked. David's opinion motivated me. The thought that I might let him or my family, or especially my parents, down . . . well, I wasn't going to let that happen. This was the big brother whose presence was taken away by a rumor that was too dangerous to answer. That was the way it was.

## Final Thoughts on Greenwood

Greenwood today is not the Greenwood of my youth. I don't believe all racism has been extinguished there—not by a long shot—nor do I think complete and equal justice has arrived for black people in Mississippi or in most places in the

United States. It surely is different, however, in the sixty years since my high school days and now.

Two contrary social movements were underway in and around my hometown: the emergence of the civil rights movement, in which African Americans resisted and protested inequality, and the increasing white resistance to the social changes happening all around them. While I was in high school, the state and the town became a hotbed of white supremacists and ugly, violent resistance to the civil rights movement.

Medgar Evers, a field secretary for the National Association for the Advancement of Colored People, was born in Decatur, Mississippi, and he first gained national notice for his investigations of the murder of Emmett Till. He worked out of the NAACP office in Jackson, Mississippi. Later, long after I had left Greenwood, the Reverend Dr. Martin Luther King Jr. did a lot of work there, visiting often with his right-hand man, Rev. Ralph Abernathy. Sometimes, King might confer with social workers, and sometimes he would preach at the church. I was at a reunion once, talking to an old acquaintance whose father was a shoe repairman, and he told me Reverends King and Abernethy and others stayed at their house when King would visit. He also told me that when King stayed over, he would go outside, and there would be a black car parked at the end of the street. That black car held FBI agents who shadowed King and his entourage wherever they went.

Greenwood was also home for a time to the assassin of Medgar Evers, Byron De La Beckwith. His crime much postdated my time in the town, but his story illustrated that in spite of all the ugly energy and unrest in the Mississippi of my childhood, we made something of ourselves. Surely, we were lucky to have the support we had, but we made the most of it against very great odds.

De La Beckwith was born in California but lived much of his life in Greenwood. After serving in World War II, he married and returned there. After the *Brown v. Board of Education* ruling in 1954, during my sophomore year in high school. We were aware of the decision, but it wasn't wise to discuss it much or openly, to show too much hope. He joined the White Citizens' Council, one of many white supremacist groups that sprang up in defiance of *Brown*. De La Beckwith is also reputed to have been a member of the White Knights of the Ku Klux Klan, the Klan's most violent wing. Mississippi was home central for the darkest forces of the Klan, and as of this writing, at a time when the Klan is largely in decline, there are still about one hundred Mississippians who count themselves members of the White Knights. The White Knights have been linked to some of the most notorious killings of the civil rights era, including the 1963 bombing of the Sixteenth Street Baptist Church in Montgomery, Alabama, killing four little girls, and the murder of three white civil rights workers near Philadelphia, Mississippi, in 1963.

De La Beckwith shot Evers in the driveway of the latter's home in Jackson in June 1963 just as Evers returned from a meeting with NAACP lawyers. Evers was carrying some T-shirts protesting Jim Crow.

As it had with Till, it took a long time to achieve justice in the Medgar Evers case. In 1964, two separate trials on the charges against De La Beckwith ended in hung juries. He was not convicted of the murder until 1994, fully thirty years later, when a jury in Jackson of eight blacks and four whites found him guilty. Appeals to the state Supreme Court took another three years, but in 1997, he was finally found guilty, by which time he had but four years to live.

It had always been there in the background, this sad, long tension between people of one color and people of another. This tension was especially concentrated, and had been for generations, in my home state of Mississippi. Few of us were unscathed by eruptions of racial hatred—it touched even my own family, when the Neros had to send their eldest son away because of a stupid, murderous rumor. Our one chance was to work hard and get out.

# CHAPTER 4

## GOOD-BYE TO THE FARM, HELLO, ADULTHOOD

One moment in our family life on the farm will stay with me as long as I live. I think of it with pride. It was a simple, quiet moment that took place when I was still a boy, sometime in 1945.

It was the end of cotton-picking season, late September perhaps. It was a hot day, and the harvest had all been taken in. We worked hard for an entire spring and summer, picking the cotton as it arose in waves. Then Daddy carried it to the gin to have it combed out and added to our bale.

On this day, Daddy drove off in the wagon with our 1,500-pound load of cotton. It was our precious yield of so much work. We hoped that he would return to us with a few bags of sweets for us in his pockets. Daddy came into the house. He proudly announced, "I just want you to know that I sold our bale for $150, and on my way back home, I stopped by and paid off the note on the farm. We own this place free and clear."

As I remember it, he poured himself a glass of lemonade, went to the porch, and sat in the swing, going back and forth a little, looking out, savoring his lemonade and the afternoon.

Mother and Daddy had been living and working on the farm for more than twenty-five years. Daddy was close to sixty at that time. Our family had worked diligently and methodically for all that time, and now he had paid off all his debts. The land was inherited, but Daddy had to take out loans for this and that over the years, using our land as collateral. He was a black man who finally owned his house and land. I doubt that Daddy ever had to borrow another penny on his property for the rest of his life. I have to wonder if many other black farmers in Mississippi can say the same.

I might have been well raised, but that did not ensure against bumps in the road, uncertainties, difficulties, or crises. My journey was from Mississippi to California, to Kentucky, and eventually, to Philadelphia. I took some detours and made a false start or two. Some of the best luck I ever had was not my doing; it was a matter of being in the right place at the right time. But I am certain that I would never have done as well as I did without the challenge and support of my family.

As each sibling came of age—David, Mary Jean, Colleen, and Clyde—they moved away to different futures. As our household got smaller, the remaining siblings continued to work with Mother and Daddy in the fields as they had always done. But our parents were nearing the end of their working lives, and soon they would have to move off the farm into more comfortable circumstances. As the 1950s matured, I went through high school worrying about what I would do with my adult life. All the children left the house one by one. I saw that our family's life on the farm was winding down.

That was when I began to have an idea that would stay with me for as long as my parents lived. I watched them still working hard into their retirement. I began to wish of building them a presentable house. How I would do that, I didn't know. But I resolved to making enough money to build them that house. Once ignited, this dream powered me through the rest of my education and advanced training.

## Different Paths

My dad and, especially, my mother had a knack for getting along with many different kinds of people. People along the way put me in leadership positions. They continued to think of me when opportunities arose. My family was empathetic to other people, and this helped me navigate numerous situations throughout my career.

Four of the five Nero children landed in places much different from the farm we had grown up on. Three of us landed on the West Coast. My sisters Colleen and Mary Jean moved to Southern California, and David lived in Oregon. Clyde was the exception; he stayed in Mississippi his whole life. I ended up in Philadelphia.

David, the eldest boy, first moved to Washington, DC. He found work there, and when he became of age, he was drafted into the army. He adapted very well, so well that he was accepted to the Officer Candidate School. He did extremely well, graduating as a second lieutenant. During World War II, he served in Europe and Northern Africa, working with the Second Cavalry Division and Ninety-Second Infantry Division, both of which were known as the Buffalo Soldiers or African American brigades.

During my brother's deployment overseas, many times a day I would see or hear my parents pray for my brother's safety. Communications were difficult and slow in those days, and there being no television or 24-7 news coverage, reports from abroad might take days to get to the States. We might hear from David once a month by letter. Thank God my brother was spared from direct combat.

At the war's end, David returned home, serving at several military locations and eventually being promoted to first lieutenant. When war broke out in Korea, he served as head of the 157th Transportation Trucking Company, where he was in charge of moving supplies to the front line. An ammunition truck in his convoy caught fire, and David had the presence of mind to evacuate the area and push the engulfed truck off the road, guaranteeing the safety of his troops. For that act of bravery, he was awarded the Bronze Star, one of about ten medals he would earn during his military career.

David told me that after the Chinese joined the North Koreans in the conflict, troops would come down in waves. He and his troops spent days retreating in the cold and ice. It was the coldest weather he had ever experienced in his life, and he did not think they would survive it. During his time in Korea, he also met a Korean woman whom he married. He achieved the rank of captain, and a few years after the war, he was honorably discharged.

David studied prelaw at Columbia College in Chicago but never got his degree. At that time, he worked for different companies and saw opportunities to be promoted quickly. I think David was always the kind who wanted to be his own boss. When I graduated from high school in 1956, he was a supervisor at Zenith Plastics, a division of 3M in Gardena, California. He soon left to start his own environmental services company in Portland, Oregon. In 1971, he was listed as president of Beak Consultants Incorporated, which provided "forestry services, including timber stand improvement, tree planting and vegetation control." David was named Small Businessman of the Year for the state of Oregon in 1973. *Jet* magazine ran a notice about him, saying that his business, Nero and Associates, "[was] a manpower-oriented firm, which also [directed] Operation Step-Up, a Model Cities program which [sought] to upgrade employment opportunities for minority group members." The company "[was] a consultant and research firm with five locations in the country." One 1975 entry for Nero Industries listed locations in Philadelphia, Los Angeles, and Washington, DC.

One of David's most important contracts was with United States Air Force Plant 42, where the U-2 spy planes were developed and departed from. It was also the place where the famous Lockheed Skunk Works was located. At that site, scientists and engineers developed the X-15 research jets and spy planes, such as the SR-71 Blackbird. For many years, David's company provided a range of services, including upkeep and other environmental maintenance. David once took me over there to see one of the spy planes take off, and it was an unbelievable experience. The plane had a very small cockpit, a single pilot, and several cameras. As it took off, it produced an earsplitting boom—it had broken the sound barrier on takeoff. Unforgettable. I also had the chance to meet one of the pilots, who told me about his amazing experiences and shared some wonderful stories.

Clyde and Mary Jean were the jokers in the family. Besides homework, the radio, and Bible reading, we didn't have much time for entertainment during our few leisure hours as a family. On the radio, we sometimes liked to listen to *The Major Bowes Amateur Hour* or shows like *The Shadow* when we could hear of them, because sometimes, there was more static than anything else. We went to the movies only rarely, and never on Sundays. On the infrequent occasions when there was some downtime and nothing to fill it, Clyde and Mary Jean would see to our entertainment. They would dress up, act skits, and altogether keep us in stitches. Mary Jean would dress up as a lady with a huge behind and huge breasts and do some funny dancing, and it was the funniest thing you could ever see. Mother would play the piano, accompanying their dances.

Colleen was the intense math student who'd cry herself to sleep if she couldn't figure out a homework problem. Following in our mother's footsteps, she became a terrific cook, and she often prepared the midday meal when we were all working in the fields. She used her talent in mathematics to make a fine career for herself. It took her to California, where she eventually had a home, a family, and an important job with the auditor's department for the state of California. She was twice married. Her first husband was a man named Daniel Hayes, who died of a heart attack. She later met and married Clarence Earl Phelps, who turned out to be a wonderful brother-in-law and father. Almost unbelievably, he too suffered a fatal heart attack. I used to kid her about it and say, "Don't you go marrying again—that poor third guy!"

My sister Mary Jean, a lovely woman, never married or had children, but you'd have thought just knowing her that she'd be most likely always to be around children and maybe have some of her own. She doted on children. Whenever little cousins or nieces or nephews were around, they would always ask, "Where's Aunt Jean? Where's Aunt Jean?" Jean ended up in California too, where she worked for years as a factory worker. In her early thirties, she had two bouts of cancer. First, she contracted muscle cancer. She was able to get treatments for that, but then she had to face colon cancer. After years of working under the stress of treatments, she finally had to stop working and was incapacitated most of her adult life. She passed away in 2009, the same year as my brother Clyde.

Colleen was the subject of one of the very few angry disagreements I ever saw between my parents. In 1948, when she graduated from high school, there was a heated discussion about where she would go. My daddy was a confirmed Methodist. A friend of my mother's, the assistant principal, in fact, of our high school, knew about Oakwood College, a women's college in Alabama run by the Seventh-Day Adventists. She was close to Colleen and wanted her to go to this school, as did Colleen herself. The lady said there was a scholarship for her to attend the school. My mother backed her up, not so much on religious grounds as on the grounds of being her daughter's advocate. She had heard about other schools, about sex parties and other goings-on, and she felt this school would be safer for her daughter. Daddy would have none of it. Such conflict was so infrequent in our family that I sort of just watched for the sheer entertainment.

In the end, Colleen did go to Alabama but only stayed about two months. She came back home and later attended Clark College in Atlanta. But she didn't thrive there either and lasted only a semester. I can sympathize with her situation because I would have my own adjustment challenges also. Colleen was a good student and a leader. She had been a valedictorian in her classes, but then again, she was a farm girl who had had one boyfriend her whole life. He had to walk out three miles to our house to see her. They would sit on the porch, with Daddy sitting on the porch with them, or just inside in door. That was how isolated we were. College life threw her into the lion's den, and at first, she couldn't handle it. As with all of us, the strength of our upbringing prevailed. After this stuttering start, Colleen eventually went to California and did very well for herself.

It's fair to say that a couple of us would have some issues getting comfortable with the outside world. Going away to college is a big step for any young person, let alone a young person who's seldom been more than a few miles away from home. We'd lived an intense, hardworking life together on the farm, and we'd all enjoyed our high school years, taking them seriously but also having our share of good fun. But just as I had to learn to adjust when I went to grade school, another adjustment came for all of us when we left the house and went to college.

Clyde had inherited our daddy's steadiness. He went to college, got an advanced degree, and got a job—boom, boom, boom. Clyde was the one homebody, so to speak, among us. He got his bachelor's degree from Rust College, a historically black college in Holly Springs, about 110 miles from Greenwood. It was a college attended by many family members. He got a degree in business, then he went to the University of Ohio for his master's degree. Clyde went into education as a teacher and principal at Riverview Elementary School in Sumner, Mississippi, a little less than 40 miles away from our home. He married Rose Ransom, a Mississippi lady, who was also a schoolteacher, and raised his family in Greenwood. Upon his return to our hometown, he was teacher and principal of Stone Street School. Among other offices, he was tax assessor and code enforcement officer for Greenwood and was very active in his church life. He volunteered at the voting booths and was also a board member at Habitat for Humanity, the American Heart Association, the American Cancer Society, and the Salvation Army. He was a family man, married to Rose for fifty years. Clyde's stability, his emphasis on family, became very important later when I finally achieved my dream of building a house for my parents. In 2009, Clyde died about ninety miles from where he was born, in Ridgeland, Mississippi.

# My Own Way

During my junior year, my close friend Charles Blackmon and I took a test allowing us to skip senior year and go directly to college. We were both accepted to Tougaloo College, a historically African American college in Tougaloo, Mississippi. My daddy, however, intervened. He wanted me to stay home, heal, and have my senior high school year. He felt I should achieve more at the high school level and not go off to college right away. I listened to him and stayed for my senior year. I played quarterback again and had a good last year in school. My father did not want me to feel defeated by my injury. He wanted me to get back out there and show myself and my mates that I could take it.

I graduated from high school with scholarships in sports and academics. I had the least thought of being a professional football player. As of 1956, there weren't too many black players playing football; every professional team by that time had one or two, but there were severe quotas, formal or informal, and true integration was slow. Few black men, unless they were a Marion Motley or a Jim Brown, were going to get a real chance. Besides, I was a quarterback, one of the "brain" positions on a football team. No black man was going to get a look as a quarterback. The few black players accepted were funneled into speed positions, like defensive back, and I was no good at that and didn't like it. I was a quarterback or nothing.

I would take a football scholarship because it would get me into college and keep me there. Mother and Daddy were not going to be able to help me much. They were busy helping my other brothers and sisters now well on their way. I got the message early that I should try for scholarships and see them as my ticket to higher education.

In my yearbook, several of my classmates congratulate me on going to Dillard University, a historically African American liberal arts university in New Orleans. Founded in 1930, it was still relatively new when my parents and I considered it. In the end, though, I opted for Tougaloo College.

It was not a success at Tougaloo. The main problem was the football team. I was there on a football scholarship and was expected to play, but the football program was very disappointing. That's putting it lightly. It was in disarray, and the team was terrible. Once I got there, I found out that they had lost one game 106-0 the year before. So eventually, I called my daddy and asked his permission to leave Tougaloo.

He wasn't happy. Tuition at Mississippi schools was either free or negligible, especially with the scholarships, if I would use them.

"I'm worried about you," he told me. "I want you to complete your education." In this, as in all things, he was being consistent. This was what he and my mother had stressed to all of us all along. I could see his anxiety about me. I was the youngest child, pretty much on my own, and he and my mother were near the end of their earning lives. So we came up with a plan. I would go out to Southern California and live with my sister Mary Jean in South Central Los Angeles. I could stay at her house, work, and attend college part-time. The college was conveniently situated a few blocks from her home. My dad agreed, and he drove me to the bus station to catch the bus to California. On the drive there, I swore to him that I would work hard to complete my education.

That was one of the toughest days of my life. My dad, who was so strong, was crying as I got on the bus, and I had never seen him cry before. I think I cried all the way to California.

The college I attended was George Pepperdine College, later known as Pepperdine University. During that time, Pepperdine was not located on that splendid, sunstruck campus way up in the hills overlooking the Pacific Ocean. It hadn't moved up there yet. It was affiliated with the Church of Christ, and the school was only nineteen or twenty years old at that time. It had a nice campus on the corner of West Seventy-Ninth Avenue and South Vermont Avenue, in a neighborhood called Vermont Knolls.

In 1956, South Central Los Angeles was a diverse neighborhood in transition. It was a place where black middle- and working-class families moved to find housing after World War II, which ended a decade prior. African Americans returning from the war looked for opportunities in what many hoped would be a changing US social environment. For most of the 1950s, there was work in Los Angeles. I was there well before the troubles struck that area in the mid-1960s, when the Watts riots and other civil rights–related disturbances happened. Both of my sisters lived there, and it was close to Pepperdine, the University of Southern California, and other schools. It wasn't a bad place or time to be there. While I was there, Clyde and David also came out to support and encourage me. All five of us dressed up for some good-looking group photos. We looked so sophisticated, so urban, and with it, you'd never know that only a few years after, all of us had earned our calluses picking cotton and tending animals on the farm.

California was different. I tried to work hard and tried to do my best. I took a science major, but my work was only average or less than average. Part of the problem was my need to earn money to get by. I worked on campus, doing janitorial work in the science building, and I also had a part-time job in the post office during the evenings. That left me little time for study, and it also left me pretty tired during the day, when I needed to be at my sharpest for my courses.

It's also true that although I had an encouraging and nurturing high school experience, I discovered that there was a big gap between my preparation back in Mississippi and what was expected at Pepperdine. So although I did complete a fair number of credits, I struggled academically.

Meanwhile, I tried to keep up my football skills because I was hopeful of using my football scholarship somewhere. Pepperdine had a football program, but it had seen its best days, and it was going to get shut down in just a few more years. I think the team was 2-5 or something like that the year I was there. Remember too that I was still recovering from my broken leg. I'd gotten through my senior year in high school with the special brace, and I'd managed not to break it again at Tougaloo. I didn't play at Pepperdine. I sort of had my eye on the University of Southern California. On many afternoons, I'd go down to Exposition Park, a big beautiful park near my sister's house, and throw the football to keep my skills up and challenge my leg. I made some friends there, including some boys who played football at USC. They encouraged me to try out for the team, so I kept that idea in the back of my mind. Eventually, I scraped together enough money to buy a used 1954 MG convertible. I thought of it as my dream car.

One set of skills I didn't put to very good use was my academic skills. I'd always gotten good grades, as you know, and it was frustrating to realize that I had a lot of ground to make up for. Perhaps it was because of being so far from home. It was certainly a different world. I wasn't the only black man on campus, but there weren't an overwhelming number of us. Perhaps it was all that sunshine and all those pretty girls. My teachers saw potential in me and told me so but were disappointed by my performance.

I don't know whether it was a crisis of confidence, but at Pepperdine, I looked around me at all my fellow students from different parts of the country. I will say that there might have been ten black students, including athletes, in all of Pepperdine. That didn't help my sense of being in a very distant, different, intimidating place. When I looked at other students and I compared their levels of preparation to mine, their skills, their basic life experiences, their expectations, I started to question whether I had what it took. Mathematics told the story. Some of the students around me behaved as if math were a second language for them. In high school, I had gotten a pass in my math classes. When I broke my leg, my teacher, who was also a football coach, let me advance. So I had a lot to make up for. I tried to work hard, but I had taken on a lot of changes and a lot of outside work all at the same time.

So it wasn't long before I ended up in Dean Earl V. Pullias's office, talking about my disappointing marks. Dean Pullias was encouraging, but he said he also wondered why such an obviously bright young man wasn't doing well. I was unable to tell him, because I didn't know myself.

"What do you think the issue might be?" Dean Pullias asked.

I explained that I was working multiple jobs. I thought that might be one of the reasons.

"Well, perhaps you should give up those jobs and concentrate on your studies," he said.

Then it all came out. I talked about my grave concerns about my parents. They were getting older, and after a life dedicated to work and raising us children, they deserved a better home at a time in their lives when they could still enjoy it. I told the dean about my plan to build them a house someday. This had already become a fixed idea in my mind.

Dean Pullias was clearly moved. But he then made a point that, in retrospect, was wise advice. He told me gently, "Why, Ben, that's a beautiful idea! But you know, your parents have only you in mind. They don't expect you to do a thing like that. Perhaps you should think less about doing something for your parents and think of doing something for yourself. That's what they would want. They would want you to get a good education and be successful."

This happens to a lot of young people. Transitions are difficult, and many of us have to go down several different paths until we find the right one. After only one year, I decided to leave Pepperdine and start over. I enrolled for a brief time at USC, on the recommendation of those two Southern Cal players I'd met in the park. I wanted to try out for the football team and went in to speak to the coach. I was confident in my punting and passing skills. All the coach wanted to talk about was speed. He was sizing me up for a speed position, and I knew there was no way I could qualify.

Here was where my first lucky break came in. I heard that Coach Paul Thomas, my high school football coach, had just become an assistant coach at Kentucky State College in Frankfort, the state capital. I wrote him a letter asking whether he thought I might have a chance at qualifying for a scholarship. He wrote me back, saying, "Come on out. I know what you can do, and I will put in a word for you with the head coach, but I think you will be fine."

I still had some eligibility left on my football scholarship, but I'd lose some if I transferred all my credits to another school, which would then have to count me as a second-year student rather than a new, entering student. I had completed some college credits at Pepperdine and Southern Cal, so I left those credits behind and went to Kentucky State College to start over again.

Kentucky State wasn't Kentucky State University yet. That would come in 1972. In fact, it had been called Kentucky State College for Negroes until 1952, when the last two words were dropped. As of 1958, when I got there, it was still a largely but not exclusively black college. I guess I still had some growing up to do, because once again, as had happened at Tougaloo, I didn't get along with the head football coach, Joe Gilliam Sr., father of son Joe, who became a quarterback for the Pittsburgh Steelers and the first African American quarterback to start a season opener for an NFL team, so I didn't play football my first year. Here's why.

In the summer of 1958, I was working out with the football team, trying to qualify for my football scholarship, and I must say, I thought I was doing pretty well in working my way into the lineup. But then came the fateful day of Bull in the Ring.

Bull in the Ring is an old-time football drill that's now banned in many programs due to injuries. It sure was a favorite, though, one Coach Gilliam liked to do to test the agility and toughness of his players. It was also, if you ask me, pretty dumb. Here's how the drill worked. A number of defensive linemen were arranged in a circle. In the center of this circle was a player, on his stomach, carrying a football. When the whistle blew, a lineman would be assigned to charge the ballcarrier, who would not know where the next tackle would come from. It was a test of reactions and evasive ability since you'd get hit sooner or later from an angle you probably didn't have time to anticipate. It could be pretty brutal. I had seen drills like this before, of course, but usually for running backs. At the beginning of practice, a player I knew pretty well from Mississippi, a running back trying out for a football scholarship, was told to get in the center. He got a brutal hit, broke his ankle, and was sent home without a scholarship. So there was one man's college football career, ruined.

I had no desire to be in the center. And I didn't think, being a quarterback, that I'd have to get in there. Then, to my shock, my name was called. Why would a quarterback be subjected to Bull in the Ring? Yes, quarterbacks had to carry the ball sometimes, but it didn't make sense to subject them to a hard-hitting drill like that. I told the coach I wouldn't go.

"If you can't practice for me, then you can't play for me," he told me.

I walked off the field. Without the football scholarship, my rather slight safety net was shredded. I'd have no way to pay for my schooling at Kentucky State. After a desolate few hours, I found a phone, called my parents, and told them what had happened. They surprised me by saying, "Stay there. We'll do what we can to cover your tuition for the first year. Just stay where you are, work hard, and do your best."

It still makes me feel badly, but at the same time, it renews my sense of love and obligation. They were living close to the poverty line, were already helping out my other siblings, and now were burdened with an unanticipated expense. But they did it somehow. At the end of the summer, I was able to register for classes. I had almost nothing left over, but the important point was I had registered. I planned to make money on the side somehow with odd jobs.

On the first Sunday of the school year, I went into the Student Union Building and saw a poster inviting students to try out for a play. Don't ask me why, but I decided to audition. Maybe it was the absence of football from my schedule. I can't remember exactly what motivated me. As I've discussed, I had good friends, Charles Blackmon and Morgan Freeman, who were good actors. I had done a little drama after football season in high school, but nothing serious.

To my surprise, I landed the second male lead: Joe McCall in *The Tender Trap*. It was the same role Frank Sinatra played in the movie, which had come out a few years before. It was a full-length, three-act play, and on the basis of my efforts, somebody decided to give me a one-year drama scholarship. That would help get me through that first year at Kentucky State. I became a member of the Kentucky Players, the college drama team, and I did the three-act play in the fall and two one-act plays in the spring.

It's a little humorous that I should get such a scholarship. I realize I had praised Mrs. Williams, my high school drama teacher, and she certainly was responsible for bringing out what little thespian talent I had. Plus, as I've said, such training was really training for being an adult in public life, so it stood me in good stead in that indirect way. But the fact is, drama was not my favorite endeavor. I would much rather run onto a football field on Saturdays and get beaten up there than endure going onstage in front of hundreds of eyes and act a part. Mrs. Williams in high school knew what I could do, and she assigned me the parts for which she thought I had some aptitude. My schoolmate Morgan Freeman, as everyone knows, could do anything, comedy or drama. He was good at it all. I was good, if anything, at only the serious stuff; I couldn't really play comic parts. To be honest, I didn't like it the way Morgan did. He loved it, and it really was not my thing. But I did act that first year at Kentucky State and again was given roles that suited my ability and personality. The scholarship helped me get through the year and made sure I did not have to lean any harder on the generosity of my poor parents.

The other piece of luck was that Coach Gilliam, the one with whom I had my little run-in, hit a patch of bad luck. In his two years at Kentucky State, his teams had a record of two wins, thirteen losses, and one tie. Now, he'd go on to a stellar coaching career with Tennessee State University, where he would enjoy several national titles. My good luck was that he was let go at the end of my freshman year. In fact, in the spring of 1959, the entire football staff was let go, except lone assistant coach, Robert "Plug" Williams. A new head coach, Kentucky-born Sam B. Taylor, was brought in. He'd been coaching at Bluefield State in West Virginia for most of the decade, and before that, he had a stellar record as a coach and educator. I want to mention that he had helped desegregate Kentucky public schools after the *Brown v. Board of Education* Supreme Court ruling had come down in 1954.

I recall crossing the intramural field that morning on the way back from classes to my dormitory when I passed close by the office of Rufus B. Atwood, the president of Kentucky State. To my surprise, Mr. Simmons, assistant to President Atwood, came up to me and said, "The president would like to see you in his office."

President Atwood had arranged a nice little meeting with me, Plug Williams, the one surviving assistant coach, and Coach Taylor, the new head coach.

Plug Williams gestured to me and told Coach Taylor, "There's your quarterback right there."

In the meantime, I acted a little bit and worked hard to keep my grades up. I was attracted to the sciences, and I made sure not to let my marks sag as I had at Pepperdine. I wanted it to stick this time, and I'd do anything to make sure of it.

I tried out for the football team again in the spring, and the new coach recognized me as his quarterback. That would lead to three years of playing college football as starting quarterback and three years of a scholarship, which would help defray some of the costs of college life. As you'll see, I had to show some resources and ingenuity in finding jobs to make ends meet. But I had begun, little by little, to piece it all together.

I had a biology major, with minors in chemistry and English. As with many college students in their first and second years, I was trying to figure out what I would do, what career I would follow. It wasn't going to be acting, that was for sure, and it wasn't going to be football. I had spoken to a Dr. Lane back home in Greenwood, who had talked with me about the difficulties and rewards of being a physician, and I had met a football coach who also was a dentist and told me about his work. Both career paths had attracted me back then because they would help me fulfill my parents' hopes that I'd go into a profession.

So I followed what I had always loved, and I began to think broadly about a science- or medicine-related career, some kind of health-care profession. The courses were challenging, but I felt comfortable and, in general, performed more to my ability than I had at either Tougaloo or Pepperdine.

My college years were full of variety, as college should be. I kept growing up, unbeknownst to myself, and was accepting that people weren't the same and had different backgrounds and different attitudes and expectations. I made friends and was fairly popular. Being a quarterback didn't hurt. And I had my moments at Kentucky State.

One year—1960, I believe it was—we went down to play Morris Brown College, a historically African American college in the Atlanta area. We always beat Morris Brown pretty badly, but this particular time, we gave them an especially terrific whomping. I had a great day, throwing all sorts of touchdown passes. The local newspaper, it might have been the *Atlanta Daily World*, ran the perhaps inevitable headline the next day: NERO FIDDLES WHILE MORRIS BROWN BURNS.

Football was different then. It wasn't the near-professional sport it is today, training methods were not the superpower, year-round affair they have become, and the dominance of African American players in the game was only just beginning. Some of us were hoping we'd catch on with a pro team afterward, and some of my teammates did get recruited. As you'll see, I even went out to Los Angeles for a somewhat-abortive tryout. Almost all the rest of us knew it was mainly a means of getting ourselves through school on a scholarship. For a lot of us, it was being able to afford Kentucky State or going back home.

I was also a fair tennis player, but not very good at basketball. Not everyone liked me—that's going to happen—and I had to learn to roll with it. Maybe these people disliked me because I didn't talk like them or act like them. At a small college like that, differing backgrounds could clash. Being from Mississippi didn't always make you friends in Kentucky or anywhere else. I was respected, however. I was known for being a good and serious student and an athlete.

In those days, the civil rights movement was in full swing in the South. People on campus talked about it a fair amount, but we didn't have outright unrest that I recall. I was active with many other students in civil rights activity, participating in several sit-ins and demonstrations. One thing Kentucky State did have was conferences during the summer. Southern churches, many of which were the most vibrant centers of the movement for social change, would have frequent conferences on our campus. I think the Reverend Dr. Martin Luther King Jr. was there at one time, and I know Reverend Abernethy was.

Kentucky State is way up on a bluff overlooking the city of Frankfort proper, which is down in the valley by the Kentucky River. We were not allowed to have cars on campus. A few years before I got to Kentucky State, a black student had been accused of raping a white woman, and he had a car. Thus the ban. Since I wasn't able to have it, I sold my 1954 MG convertible and used the money to pay for clothes and other expenses.

One person exempt from this ban was a friend of mine, Sam Price, who happened to be a military veteran. I took physics courses during the summer so I wouldn't have to take them in the fall, when I was playing football. Sam was taking summer courses at the same time. That was where we met and became friends.

Money remained an issue. My parents had helped as much as they possibly could, and I had to find ways to earn some cash. Some of these ways make me smile to remember.

Sam had a car he was allowed to drive on campus. The bus and taxi service from Frankfort up to the college was very poor. So we had the bright idea of starting an informal ferry service, picking up delegates to the church conferences and driving them up the hill to their accommodations in the student dorms. As it happened, Sam was taking courses in the afternoons, and I was taking courses in the mornings. So that determined our shifts in this ferry service we set up: Sam took mornings, and I took afternoons.

We went down into town and picked up delegates and their luggage as they arrived by bus or train and drove them back up the hill to the college. Most of these delegates were ladies, the most wonderful, generous, appreciative ladies we had ever met. They thought it was so wonderful that these lovely young black college students were driving them up and taking care of their luggage, and they would tip you for carrying their luggage and bringing them up the hill. Sometimes they'd tip you $20. Can I tell you how much money that was back then? That was unheard of—that's how much. I thought I was going to go crazy with all that money. I didn't know where I was going to put it. I paid my friend for gas and saved the rest. Conferences might last a week or two, and I began to think of myself as one of the richer guys in the world.

During the evenings, when not studying, I was a short-order cook at the student grill, where you could get hamburgers and hot dogs. There, I again encountered these delegates to the conferences, and they would give tips that were incredible because they were happy to see black kids in college that were doing something for themselves. I'll never forget these ladies.

I made myself available for all sorts of odd jobs. Back in those days, you actually could just about work your way through college, and many of us students did.

In the springtime, I cleaned houses and did spring-cleaning for people. I told the office of the dean of students, "Whenever somebody calls and needs somebody to come and do spring-cleaning, please place my name first on the list." I went and washed windows, did floors, cleaned up yards, trimmed trees, burned trash and clippings—whatever was needed—for a dollar an hour, which was fine with me.

The Kentucky Derby Festival came along for two weeks at the end of April, with the Derby on the first Saturday in May. I went and parked cars, waited tables, or did room service at hotels during Derby time. One weekend there, I made $1,500. I could hardly be controlled after that. I was never wealthy, of course, but I made it through.

In my senior year, an interesting thing happened that shows you where the nation was at that time. Some of the football players on the college team were getting invitations from professional clubs to come try out. One of my roommates, John Kennerson, a tackle, was drafted by the Los Angeles Rams. He got to play in a few games for them in the 1960 season. I myself was invited to a tryout in 1960 by the Los Angeles Chargers. The Chargers were part of the new American Football League. This would be their only year in Los Angeles; they'd move down to San Diego and have a successful record right through to 1970, when the AFL merged with the National Football League. For the Chargers, 1960 would be a very good year, with a 10-4 record, a division championship, and a near loss in the league championship game.

I went to Los Angeles to see what would happen. What I saw was the same old thing. Once I got to camp, Sid Gillman, the great coach of the Chargers, told me right away that I'd be getting a tryout at cornerback—exactly what I did not want. I was a quarterback and just wasn't cut out for defensive positions. I didn't have the skills or the speed. It was, really, what had been happening for a while to promising black football players: no matter the position in which you might have excelled in college, no matter how poised or smart you were, you weren't going to be allowed to try out for a leadership position, a "brainy" position, such as quarterback. You were shoved into speedy defensive positions, and for me, as for many other players, that just wasn't going to work. But my visit was fun, and I got a look at how the pros operated.

As I was completing my degree, I started looking around for the next step. My vision of some health-care-related career was starting to firm up, and it looked like it might be dentistry. I found out about a post at the University of Kentucky in Lexington. Those accepted would be trained as histopathology technicians for dental pathologists. So I applied and was accepted. I was trained in the medical school with the medical pathology technicians. I learned to cut and stain tissues and create slides for the pathologists to read. You start with the dental tissue to be prepared, then you dehydrate it, embed it in a paraffin medium, and once that is set, you can cut superthin sections of it on a machine known as a rotary microtome. These cuts, very delicate, are washed, put on a glass slide, and dried overnight. Then they are stained, dried once again, and mounted on a slide. Once mounted, they are ready for the dental pathologists to view them beneath a microscope. It's a painstaking, time-consuming process. That class would be an enormous help in my future studies and career, in two ways, both in my later work as an orthodontist and because it helped me earn a little extra money while I was attending dentistry school.

While I was working as a histopathology technician, my boss was Dr. Sheldon Rovin. Meeting and working with him formed a professional friendship that was very important to me. I didn't know it, but he was about to become my adviser, shepherding me through the next stage of my studies.

Encouraged, I applied to the University of Kentucky College of Dentistry, a division of the university's medical center that had just opened up in 1962. They were taking a bit of a chance on me, and in speaking with them, I could tell they were concerned about my small college background and the fact I'd played football, not the usual profile for an applicant to an advanced professional degree program. This brand-new division of the medical center was trying to—and did—attract the best candidates from all over the country. The admissions board wanted the College of Dentistry to be a reputable institution, with an emphasis on preventive dentistry, distinct from emergency dentistry, where you have to fix, extract, and reconstruct people's dentition. When most people think of dentistry, they think of the emergency procedures, but the preventive side, which helps people avoid later problems like tooth decay, is very important as well.

In some ways, and I can't blame them, they had their concerns about me. They wanted me to be sure I wanted to be there. I had some questions about that myself. They looked at me and saw a student who had gone to a smaller college on an athletic scholarship. They were also concerned about the mix of their admissions class. I was African American. Whereas Kentucky State had been largely African American, the University of Kentucky was largely white, and the cultures of the two institutions showed it. My dental school classmates were all Caucasian males, most of them from the South, although we had people from colleges and universities throughout the country. The admissions board wanted to see if we were going to get along.

They suggested that I take two undergraduate courses at night to see whether I could compete. This I did in the spring semester of 1963. I took a class in comparative anatomy and another in English literature. Even paying for those two courses took some creativity. Some of the money would come from my histopathology job at the university. Luckily, the previous fall, I also had come into some extra work. I had a friend who was in the Army Reserves. He had a job preparing slides at Central Baptist Hospital in Lexington. But in the fall of 1962, the Cuban Missile Crisis hit, the armed forces were put on alert, and he was called up. So he asked me if I could take over his job for a while. The big break was that this was a job you could do at night. I finished my job at the university around 5:00 p.m., dashed home to wash up and have a bite to eat, and then I could walk to Central Baptist Hospital, which was nearby, where I would work until midnight. So I had a little extra to pay for the classes.

I proved to the admissions board that I could do it. I got an A in the comparative anatomy course and a B in the English course. I then took a dental aptitude test, which I passed, and I was accepted into the School of Dentistry beginning in fall 1963.

At the University of Kentucky, I would be attending one of the whitest institutions I had yet encountered. Pepperdine was largely white as well, but the surrounding urban community was diverse with Asians, Hispanics, and other groups in representative numbers. The University of Kentucky would be a different story. I was the only African American in a class of forty-nine students, so I was going to stick out. But my upbringing again came to my aid. Even though the faculty members and admissions people didn't know this, the fact that I had spent a large part of my life among white people was certainly helpful to me, because I was able to get along perhaps more easily than many African American men might have at that particular time.

I am happy to report that although there were a few mixed moments here and there, I got along with everyone. I assimilated well, and my classmates were cordial and generally accepting. Here again, I have to credit the way Mother and Daddy raised me to be respectful of all and to see people first and foremost as people. I have to credit good fortune, too, in giving my family white neighbors, with whom we were in constant contact. That was, as I mentioned, a little unusual in the part of the segregated South where I grew up. At the university, I had very few problems.

At an assembly of the new class, each man was introduced by name and undergraduate school. I listened to the names of the schools to which my classmates had gone, and it was hard not to feel a little intimidated. I was up against men who had gone to better universities, who had better exposure to the sciences, better credentials than mine. These guys were tough. They knew their stuff, and they knew how to study, and they were competitors. All I had was a willingness to work harder than anybody else. But at times, in my freshman or sophomore year, I'd catch myself wondering, where am I going to be this time next year?

That first year was filled with things I had never experienced, learning challenges and organizational obstacles, but I made it through reasonably well. The first year was mostly basic science, with courses in biochemistry, physiology, genetics, anatomy, microbiology, and also introductory dentistry courses. I remember taking an exam in a biochemistry class, and I earned a grade of 25 out of 100. I stared at it and assumed, heart falling through the floor, that my entire academic career was doomed. My low grade was the result of a very stupid error on my part, in which I neglected to multiply certain of my answers by two. I was really angry at myself when I realized that, and in the next three exams, I earned good grades that allowed me to bounce back.

We started our clinical courses in the second year, and from that point on, academic matters went smoothly all the way through to the end—pretty much. I adjusted to university life and learned to adapt to its demands on my intellect and schedule. I learned a great deal at the university, and my plans began to firm up. I wanted to be a good dental professional. I wanted to go back home, to Greenwood or nearby, and practice dentistry there while my parents were still living to see it. In their honor. Beyond that, my big plan, to build my parents a house, grew firmer and firmer and seemed closer and closer to being possible.

Most of the faculty members at the School of Dentistry were fair people and ambitious. They wanted this to be the best dental school in the country, and to inculcate a professional spirit, they insisted on treating you like a doctor from the moment you entered the school. They also knew there had to be group cohesiveness, fun, and social opportunities. We had athletic events, usually softball, in which everyone, faculty members and students alike, would join in, from Dean Alvin L. Morris on down. On the field, everyone was on a first-name basis. We formed a softball team that played in the industrial league in Lexington. We did very well indeed, which helped create even greater cohesion and unity.

I've already mentioned Dr. Rovin, a Jewish professor who took me under his wing in a very professional way and made sure I got through. I recall his clean-shaven face, his thin hair, and his athletic build. He, by the way, was a pretty good shortstop. Considerate and humane, with high standards, he also had a good sense

67

of humor. In morning meetings with his staff, he'd look deadpan at all of us around the room and say, "Well, it's clear I hire the handicapped."

He didn't give me anything for free, but he kept his eye on me. I have spoken already about his encouraging way, but he also knew just when to come over and say, "Come on, let's have dinner." He was the one who told me never to complain again about the house my father built.

Dean Morris was always very good to me, as were Drs. Harry Bohannon, Stephen Dachi, James Little, Thomas Mullaney, and John Mink. Dr. Stephen Dachi, chairman of the Department of Oral Medicine and one of the most brilliant men I have ever met, was especially good to me, giving me extra histopathology work and advising me at crucial points in my journey. At one time or another, they all advised me, heartened me, and helped me on my way. It was largely through that encouragement that I grew deeply attached to this institution, an attachment that has thrived to this day.

I had good relationships with just about all my classmates, and I never had any outright incidents. I did hear some things. I was told that one of the other students was looking to pick a fight with me "just because," if you know what I mean. But that was when my classmates stepped up. They came up and said, "If this guy ever picks a fight, if anything like that ever happens, we'll be there for you." Luckily, it never came to that. They didn't have to say that, but they did, which showed their regard.

I could tell that many of my classmates probably had not had much contact at all with African American people unless it had been with laborers or domestic workers. Most of my fellow students were not, for the most part, second-generation professionals, but they were people who had lived a lot differently from the way most African Americans had lived. So they had not had much contact, and they were kind of curious about me and why I was there.

On Friday afternoons, after we'd had a tough day in classes, we often went to a local watering hole, had a beer or two, and talked about how much we hated our teachers. On one such afternoon, after we'd each had a couple of beers, one of my classmates said, "Ben, we've been wondering why you're here. We thought maybe you were either an unusually smart black man who would come in here and make all As, or we thought, maybe you were a dumb guy and would flunk all your classes but would be kept in school with federal funding to satisfy some federal diversity requirement. And we've found out that you're neither one." He was kind of happy he was able to get all that off his chest, but it had taken two or three beers to do it. I said, "Yeah, how about that? Just like you."

We had a good laugh over that. It does go to show what people's expectations were and sometimes still are. I got less grief about my race and background, in fact, than another student who happened to be Jewish.

Other attitudes came through. In 1963, in my sophomore year, President John F. Kennedy was killed. I heard people who were not unhappy about that at all. One youngster cussed "the whole thing about Kennedy" and said he was glad he was gone. At the same time, I witnessed Dean Morris weeping in public. In 1966, when all-white Kentucky lost the NCAA Men's Basketball championship to the all-black starting five from what was then Texas Western, the next day in class I heard, "Well, Ben, we guess *you're* happy!" They were incensed.

Basketball was involved in another very awkward moment in 1966. University of Kentucky basketball coach Adolph Rupp, one of the greatest coaches in the history of the college game, as of 1966, had won one NIT national title, four NCAA national titles, and had taken the team to twenty NCAA tournaments.

Over at the School of Dentistry, I might as well have been on Mars for all the likelihood my path ever would have crossed that of Coach Rupp. I was in the hallway when somebody from the dean's office came up to me. "Ben, could you come over and come have lunch with Mr. Rupp?" I knew who Mr. Rupp was, so I thought I'd better go over. I didn't even take off my dentist's gown. I just went.

I found Mr. Rupp sitting with a black gentleman. I came to understand that this gentleman was the father of a tall young man, Butch Beard by name, from Breckinridge County High School in Kentucky. Butch was not there, but he was surely the subject and object of the meeting. Mr. Rupp was trying to recruit Butch for the University of Kentucky basketball team. Mr. Rupp sat with us, speaking mostly to me. With increasing unease, I noticed he said next to nothing to Butch Beard's dad. I was there, clearly, as a token black man to show the senior Mr. Beard that there were other black men on campus, black men who were excelling at the professional schools. Mr. Rupp, an enthusiastic cattle breeder, said to me at one point, "Doctor, where are you from?"

"I'm from Mississippi, Mr. Rupp."

"They got some mighty fine cows down there." And that was it.

I can't say I resented the position I'd been put in. Once I was there, I was there, and all I could do was be civil. Maybe Butch got the signal that Kentucky had a ways to go in the way it saw black people. I don't know. Butch did not come to Kentucky. He went to Louisville instead and had a good career, winning an NBA title with the Golden State Warriors and being selected as an All-Star in 1972.

To be honest, money was a much bigger issue for me than race relations. Working was frowned upon for College of Dentistry students. Understandably enough, the faculty of the brand-new and ambitious institution wanted students to devote themselves wholly to their courses. On the other hand, I had to earn extra money just to stay there. It was always a close call. The tuition wasn't overwhelmingly much, but it was more than we had. You had to buy instruments and books; you had to have a place to live in—it was always more. My first year in dental school, I lived in a house where mostly international students lived, they and their families. There was one kitchen and one bathroom. My room had only a couch, and I strung a cord across the room to hang my clothes on. I slept on the couch, head on one arm of the couch, feet on the other.

The next year, I got married. She was a country girl from a coal-mining family in Harlan County, Kentucky. The university had housing for married students, and she and I moved into an efficiency. That was all we could afford. She worked at IBM. We had a couch we let out into a bed every night, and that was pretty much the best we could do. That was my sophomore year.

One of my moneymaking efforts came thanks to my training in dental histology. Remember, I had done that training in how to cut and stain dental tissues. And thank goodness, one of my professors, Dr. Stephen Dachi, learned of my training and sought me out. He told me he was doing a research project for the Eli Lilly and Company, testing the effects of some kind of cavity liner on teeth. He brought me some tissues to cut and prepare. He would pay me $500 to cut the block and make slides out of the cuts. He had three or four blocks to do, and that was another $1,000–$1,500, a very considerable and welcome sum. It took a while, and I did it on a part-time basis.

I was friends with a classmate of mine, Kenneth Snawder—Smedley, as we called him, based on the character from the comic strip *Chilly Willy*. We applied to jobs at the Trane Company, an air-conditioning company in Lexington. We told them quite a story: We had moved to Lexington from Louisville and were trying to get ourselves established to make some money so we could bring our families along to live with us. It sounded great, and not a word of it was true. The boss said, "Well, you have to take an exam." We said "Fine." But we decided that when we took the exam, we didn't want to score too highly because it would give us away. So we made 75s or so when we probably could have gotten 100s. We wouldn't have been the first people to play dumb to get work.

They hired us, and we worked there for a month. Our original intent was to work there after school in the summer. But no, they wanted us right away, or we couldn't have the job. So thinking quickly, we said, "Can we get the late shift?" We asked because, being in dental school, we couldn't work during the day. And our bosses at Trane said, "Sure, you can have the graveyard shift."

Picture two dental students who go home after school, do their studies, then report to the Trane Company and work 11:00 p.m. to 7:00 a.m. We'd go home again, grab a quick shower and some breakfast, and get to classes. Goodness, we'd be tired. My friend's job was to go inside a big air-conditioning unit and make some repairs. He went in one night and went to sleep. They threatened to fire him for it. Only his abject apology prevailed over them.

One day, very close to the end of term, almost to the finish line, something happened that blew my cover. We were taking final exams, and I came to a question that I had to think about. So I stopped, propped my head up, and fell asleep.

The professor came up and said, "Ben, what's going on?"

I startled awake. "Oh, nothing, I was just thinking."

"No, something else is going on," he said. "Let's go into my office."

I followed him to the office, all while the exam was going on, and he repeated his question. And I had to tell him.

"You call them over there right now and tell them you quit the job," he said. "You can't do that. You have to take these exams. What do you think you are doing?"

We had only two weeks to go, and we would have been in good shape. I still have my class photo, the University of Kentucky College of Dentistry class of 1967, forty very serious young men ready for rewarding careers. I'm in the bottom row. I'm pretty easy to pick out. My diploma is one of the most precious documents I possess.

Less serious, but still an honor, was my acceptance into the Honorary Order of Kentucky Colonels. Since 1885, the Colonels have been an honorary society that has distinguished itself through social service and fund-raising for good causes. I believe Muhammad Ali had just been inducted, and my friend and classmate R. Marion Minyard nominated me. I have always been proud to be a Colonel.

As I mentioned, my original idea had been to return to Mississippi and set up a practice there. But the more I thought about it, the more I realized that my training at the university, although excellent, might not have prepared me for the kind of dentistry that I'd encounter when I got back home. So I went to my adviser, Dr. Rovin, for advice.

"I've learned so much here," I began, "but I wonder whether I am going to be successful practicing this kind of dentistry in Mississippi. Down there, I expect I'm going to be doing a lot of extractions, a lot of dentures, partials, fillings, and that's not what we've been taught here. We've been taught preventive dentistry, which is wonderful, but I'm thinking that there will be more calls in Mississippi for these other kinds of things, and I think I need a little bit more training in them."

I'd been thinking about what I'd seen growing up and how many people, because they didn't have the money or, really, enough knowledge about dental hygiene, never went to the dentist until it was too late or past too late. Or at all. You have to be a well-informed person to practice preventive dentistry for yourself or to see a dentist to have it done. And you had to have the money for it. Preventive dentistry just wasn't too much of a concept where I came from. But I wanted to go back and honor my parents, and I'd started to think about what I was likely to see among my patients.

I didn't realize a turning point was about to happen in my life. One day, Dr. Dachi said, "Well, if you want to get some added training, I did an internship at the Dental College at Albert Einstein Medical Center in Philadelphia, and if you wanted to go there, I would recommend you." I had never been to Philadelphia. It seemed like some legendary place far away. It was. But I did apply there, Dr. Dachi did recommend me, and I got in.

That was when I called up my brother David and told him that, after my degree at Kentucky State and a second one at the University of Kentucky, I was going for even more training. Maybe he was fooling, but he joked and said, "You mean to tell me you could practice dentistry tomorrow, put out your shingle, and start up making money, but instead, you're going for more training?" Maybe he was just ribbing me and was actually pretty impressed with my foresight. Looking back, I'm sort of impressed with it, if that isn't bragging too much. It certainly turned out well.

That was one of the best moves I ever made. It allowed me to get that emergency-type dentistry experience I would have needed had I ever actually gone back to Mississippi to practice. It also allowed me to be in a position to accept the next big stroke of luck when it came.

I just think I've been very fortunate in being in the right place at the right time, and in that regard, life has been very good to me. I just thank God for every opportunity I've had.

# CHAPTER 5

## PHILADELPHIA AND NOW

From time to time, my mother would say to one of her children, "Come walk with me." I remember the many times she and I walked across our land, sometimes quiet, sometimes talking things over. Each of us knew every inch of that land. All of us had worked every inch of it. Fifty-one acres was a lot of land; it was our world, and it sustained my parents and my family for a half-century. It was hard to walk across it without thinking of harvests past, playing catch, cutting wood, doing chores, or of brothers and sisters who were there and now gone, of all of us working as a family. Every step of it was pregnant with memories of our lives together.

Very occasionally, Mother called me out for a walk when there was a question or a worry of some kind. Mostly, though, I think Mother asked me to take these walks just to have some time with me. Sometimes she had something to say; other times, she just wanted to hear what was on my mind. Maybe, increasingly as the time neared for me to leave the farm and strike out on my own, she just wanted to have me close for a little while and hear my voice. When I got into my high school years, there were times when I'd rather have been out with my friends or perhaps talking to some girl, but I wasn't going to disrespect my mother.

As I write this, I have lived more than twice as much of my life in the Philadelphia area as I ever did in Mississippi. You can take the man out of the state, but you can't take the state out of the man. I know I am still a Mississippi Nero deep down who grew up in Greenwood and had many of my formative moments there. All those walks with my mother helped. I am sure it helped shape me in ways it would be hard to trace today. They were lessons in thoughtfulness, in intimacy, most of all in being loved.

It's also true that I have come a long way. Somehow, I got advanced degrees and training that led to a long career as an orthodontist in one of America's biggest cities. In some of the institutions in which I studied—the University of Kentucky School of Dentistry and, later, at the Albert Einstein Medical Center—I would be the first African American graduate. I was the only African American orthodontist in the Philadelphia region for many years, one of the very few such orthodontists in the country. Most of my patients have been African American, and many of them have been in dental and/or financial straits, and I have tried to help them with both. I am now seeing the grandchildren of patients I first treated thirty or forty years ago. That's right: I have treated some families over three generations. I've heard a lot of stories and told my share.

Nearing eighty as I write, I am the last surviving member of my siblings. I still stay in touch with many other Neros in Mississippi and elsewhere. I make long-distance phone calls every week to old classmates and acquaintances. I am a faithful attendee at class reunions in Greenwood, as our little class of fewer than fifty students dwindles with time. I also remain active at my various alma maters. I never did go back to Greenwood to practice dentistry, but I hope and believe that I managed to fulfill and perhaps exceed what my parents expected of me.

I was getting some great advice from Dr. Dachi at the University of Kentucky. I could hardly believe it when I was accepted for the internship at Albert Einstein, but off I went to Philadelphia. In the fall of 1967, I began what I thought would be a year at the Albert Einstein Medical Center, an esteemed institution that started as the Jewish Hospital for the Aged, Infirm, and Destitute in the 1860s, with the charge of treating poor people of all religions. Through the years, it changed and grew, taking on Einstein's name in 1952. As I write, it is both one of the nation's great medical training institutions and also a multicenter health-care system employing about 8,500 people.

Philadelphia and the experience of being a resident at Einstein was something else again. I'd seen cities by that time, of course, having lived in Los Angeles, Frankfort, and Lexington, but I was about to settle for good, although I couldn't have known that at that time, in a truly diverse city during a time of rapid social change, the 1960s. It was not an easy move. My wife, who was really more comfortable living in a small town, was not thrilled about moving to Philadelphia. She also wanted to start a family, and I certainly couldn't blame her, but it was something I wasn't ready for until I had established myself in my profession. I was trying to accomplish something very difficult, as I had been for the previous seven years, graduating from a college and a graduate program, working extremely hard, making up ground I didn't know I had lost back in high school, taking whatever jobs I could to make ends meet. I was about to step up to the next level, whatever that would be.

At Einstein, a huge part of the residency was being on call. Professionally, this was our baptism of fire. We were regularly assigned long hours on call, during which we had to take any patients that came our way, and in a big, socioeconomically diverse town like Philadelphia, you were likely to see just about everything. I knew I couldn't do only what was expected; somehow, I had to do more. I was willing to study harder, work harder, take midnight calls, which the other residents were happy to let me do, anything to finish in good standing. The work was the most difficult I'd ever done. I got good experience of the emergency dentistry I had come there to master. Located in an urban environment, with a huge population to draw from, the program threw at us anything we were ready for and some things we weren't.

I also was learning so much more that excited me about my profession. I was really loving what I was learning. I was loving it so much that I decided to ask about the possibility of joining the full residency program in orthodontics the next year. As my brother David told me, quite incredulously, I didn't need four more years. I could hang out my shingle and practice dentistry at any time. But the more I learned, the more I saw patients with all manner of dental needs in such a challenging clinical environment, the more I felt drawn to professional study in orthodontics. The three-year residency at Einstein would be the way to gain the expertise and credentials I'd need.

Of course, the answer was no. Residencies at Einstein were and are coveted and very competitive. At that time, Einstein took only three residents in orthodontics every other year. I might be an intern, but I had no special entrée. I was told all positions for residencies were taken.

This was disappointing, but not devastating. My wife probably heard the news with some relief. Besides, after my internship, I would be very well qualified to begin a dental practice anywhere in the country.

One of the three men recently accepted into the Einstein program had a somewhat lackadaisical approach to his residency. He often approached me, intern that I was, and asked me to fill in for him on his nightly on-call hours. He also did a few other things that the very exacting staff at Einstein didn't like. In the spring, he was disinvited from the program. Einstein called and told me that there was an opening if I wanted it. I called Dr. Rovin at Kentucky.

"I've been offered a residency here," I told him. "Do you think I should take it?"

"I don't know much about it," he said. He encouraged me to call a friend of his who was now the head of the Orthodontics Department at the University of Pennsylvania. I did, and he said simply, "Take it. It's a good program."

In 1967, I began at Einstein. My superiors and supervisors had an air of skepticism about me, but I'd encountered that before. If I made it through—a big *if* in the minds of some of the administrators—I would be the first African American graduate of the orthodontics program, a highly technical specialty employing some of the most advanced techniques in dentistry. I'd be starting the program at thirty years old. They were giving me a chance. I had to think some of it has to do with my willingness to take whatever work came my way, make midnight calls when other interns couldn't, even take other interns' shifts. I hope that my Nero ability to get along with a wide range of people was in there too; it certainly came into play once I started my practice. At any rate, of course I accepted the offer, and it was one of the best decisions I ever made.

It proved final, however, for our marriage. She had been able to transfer from her IBM job in the Frankfort area up to an IBM office in Philadelphia. But all the changes and pressures of moving, my long hours away from home, and so on were factors in the end of our marriage. She and I stayed in cordial touch for many years, and as it happened, she stayed in the Philadelphia area.

Let me say something about the relative novelty of a nationally recognized postgraduate training program in orthodontics circa 1970. Orthodontics was and is an elite specialty. Practitioners traditionally had been trained by family members or a preceptor; training, that is, was acquired within an informal but time-honored apprenticeship system rather than at a college or university. But after World War II, as the middle class grew and demand for orthodontic services increased, more and more dental schools added orthodontics programs. This was yet another way in which I was lucky to be where I was and when. I got to the University of Kentucky just as it was starting its dental college, and here I was, entering the Albert Einstein program in orthodontics, a program that had not been in existence too long and was already one of the most eminent in the country.

I went from being head intern to, once again, having to work extremely hard. I had stepped into a situation where my fellow residents came in with training and preparation somewhat superior to mine, and I had to work that much harder to meet the standards of the program. One good example: I was never a good writer and had to work as hard as I could to produce documents with clarity, precision, and correctness. The chief of the program, Dr. Maxwell S. Fogel, was hard on me for the entire length of my stay at Einstein. It was pressurized, competitive, and demanding.

One factor was the great difference in culture between the programs at the University of Kentucky and Einstein. At Kentucky, my classmates and I enjoyed a collegial relationship with our faculty advisers. They drove us hard and held us to high expectations, but they also liked to take us to dinner and play league softball together. They did what they could to bring down the traditional wall between faculty and advanced students. As of 1970, however, at the major teaching hospitals in Philadelphia—Einstein, Temple University, and the University of Pennsylvania—things were much the opposite. Faculty kept aloof from advanced students, shunned fraternization, and insisted on hierarchy. They were in their places, and we were in ours.

When I came to Einstein as an intern, I was gung ho. I had come from Kentucky and a collegial department there. At first, I found it hard to adjust to the distance kept by faculty at Einstein. On top of this, I was going through a divorce. Often, I didn't really want to be there. At times, I was almost hoping Dr. Fogel would kick me out of the program. But he never did.

I did have the support of my fellow residents. They were working hard also, and whatever skepticism they might have harbored, if any did, when they first met me disappeared as we spent more time together. I think that at the end, when we graduated and went out to set up our practices, there was a lot of mutual admiration, as there should have been. Gradually, I found my rhythm and got some good work done.

In my third year of the residency, I met an orthodontist named Knowlton R. Atterbeary. The first African American orthodontist in Philadelphia and one of the very few in the whole country, Dr. Atterbeary had a successful practice in the Medical Arts Building in Center City on Sixteenth and Walnut Streets. He was professional, interested, encouraging, knowledgeable, and he had created a vigorous practice, all the things I wanted to be and do. We had an excellent talk and stayed in touch.

In September 1970, during my final year at Einstein, Dr. Atterbeary dropped dead suddenly of a heart attack. I remember the shock of hearing the news, but an even bigger shock was in store. Dr. Atterbeary's practice—office, staff, equipment, patients—still existed and needed an owner. Dr. Atterbeary's widow, Ida Atterbeary, offered me his practice. In fact, she was anxious for me to have it: it was a mostly African American clientele, and she was anxious to preserve this vital service and her husband's legacy. I would have to purchase it, of course.

As sad as I was about the death of Dr. Atterbeary, this proposal would be a boost for my career. If I could get permission from the department at Einstein and somehow get a loan with which to buy the practice, I could pretty much walk into a ready-made orthodontics practice in a top-five American city, all set up and waiting for me.

Those were two big *if*s. I really wanted to complete my degree because so much of my future viability depended on it; plus, I hadn't come this far not to finish it. But Dr. Atterbeary's practice required immediate attention, including the tricky issue of securing a loan.

First, I spoke to my superiors about what I should do. Dr. Atterbeary had been a member of the faculty at Einstein, and Dr. Fogel felt a degree of collegial obligation to him. He also, to his credit, had a commitment to faculty and student diversity. Plus, he respected Mrs. Atterbeary's wishes and was trying to help her out as much as he could. Further, Dr. Fogel knew that no white dentist would buy a black practice or a practice seen as black. So my superiors agreed that I should accept the offer and purchase Dr. Atterbeary's practice, even before my residency was over. But they told me I also had to complete my residency on time in the spring. By this point, it was almost as important to Einstein as it was to me that

I finish in a timely way. They were taking a chance, trying something new, and even though they were being very tough on me at times, they had a lot invested in seeing me through to completion. There was no question of affirmative action. It didn't work like that. I had shown and was determined to keep showing that I deserved to be there and could do the intellectual and professional work to prove it. Still, I'm sure several highly placed directors here and there were happy to have their first black graduate.

All this meant that, during my final year, possibly the most difficult year of a difficult residency, I would be doing not only that work but also the work of establishing myself in Dr. Atterbeary's practice. The human part of it, meeting with staff and patients, I could easily accomplish. But there was a load of paperwork and legal work in taking possession of the practice, and there was that loan.

As my colleagues and I began to get near the end of our time at Einstein, we discussed the practicalities of establishing a practice. I'd hear them say wonderful things like, "With this Einstein degree we're going to have, we've found out they'll loan you money left and right!" It was the early 1970s, and the words *affirmative action* were much in the news and on many lips. And in a jocular fashion, some of my colleagues would say, "Ben, when you get set up, you're not going to have the least problem. You're going to get start-up money a lot sooner than any of us ever will. If we were smart, we'd invest in you right now. When you decide to sell shares of your company, we'll line up to buy stock."

The reality was much harsher. I would need about $25,000, a serious sum in those days, to buy the practice. I went to the most reputable banks in Philadelphia. They all wished me well and said no. "But this isn't a ground-up proposition," I said. "I'm buying a going operation." Apparently, it didn't matter to them that the practice already existed, that all I pretty much had to do was walk right in, or that I was soon to graduate with full credentials from a prestigious institution such as Albert Einstein. It was terribly frustrating. My colleagues liked to jest that as of 1970–1971, an African American like me, a man with everything going for him, a standout, almost unique in his accomplishments and professional expectations, was a shoo-in for financial support.

I was finding out the men giving the money just did not see it that way. Whether race was involved, I do not know, although, considering everything I just outlined above, I found it hard to fathom how they could see me as a poor risk. Even today, the financial sector simply does not treat black and white equally. I realize there's an argument on the other side, that when black people come in to ask for loans, they usually have less collateral, less wealth built up, less of a track record with money. The average worth of black households in the middle class is very much lower than for white households. All that translates to a poor risk.

Granted, it was a black practice. But I doubt that was the problem. It would not have made business sense to turn down a loan to buy it. Atterbeary had excelled and had been very successful. As a business, it was healthy.

I have to think it was me. There I was, with all my diplomas and qualifications, all my technical skills, all my experience, with an established practice waiting for me in Center City, and I couldn't find a single bank that would loan me the $25,000. I appreciated that it was a lot of money—I wasn't ignoring that. I knew I would pay it back, with interest. My parents had not raised me to run away from commitments or treat business affairs lightly.

I saw my journey as proof of my trustworthiness. The bankers probably looked at me as a young man with no collateral, a man without any source of money should I experience difficulty in paying the money back. They saw where I'd come from, and while they might have congratulated me on how far I'd come, they saw *Mississippi* and *cotton farm*, and those words just did not sing to them. That outweighed whatever promise I saw in myself or others saw in me.

One banker put it to me like this: "To be very honest with you, we'd rather give a loan to an old lady who wants to start a wig shop on the corner than give it to you. At least with her, we'd know we could get federal insurance on the loan and recoup the money if and when the wig shop went bust. We have no guarantee with you."

I wasn't happy to have Dr. Atterbeary's practice, my dream, compared to some rickety wig shop. I considered myself a far stronger bet than that. But nothing prevailed.

Surely, I was not going to miss out on this wonderful opportunity just because a bunch of shortsighted bankers couldn't take me seriously enough for a loan. More than half-desperate, I went to a friend of mine, a man I'd gotten to know since I'd become a Philadelphian. He was Clarence Peaks, the running back from Michigan State drafted in the first round by the Philadelphia Eagles, for whom he played for seven years, including their NFL championship year of 1960. He played nine years in all, finishing with two years for the Pittsburgh Steelers. A man well-known throughout the city of Philadelphia, Clarence made a great success for himself after football, both as a media figure—he was a sports analyst on local stations such as WIP—and a businessman. He showed real money smarts, becoming a financial consultant and salesman of insurance and other financial instruments.

"Clarence," I told him, "I've about worn out my shoes tromping all over this town, looking for a banker to give me enough money to buy this practice. And not a single one has shown the slightest inclination." I explained the situation with Dr. Atterbeary, Einstein, and everything. "I just don't know what to do," I told him.

"You and I have known each other for a good while," Clarence said. "I tell you what, I don't need to loan you the money. Any bank in town will give it to you if I cosign the loan with you. They don't know you from Adam, but everybody knows who I am." He was right about that.

"You'd do that?"

"On one condition."

"Which is?"

"You buy some insurance from me. I have a fine selection of policies here, and I'm sure we can find one for you."

Clarence never made an easier sale. I just have to say, thank God for football! Clarence knew what he was talking about. He cosigned with me, the bank was happy to give us the money, and I bought the practice. That was a lot of money, as I know very well, and Clarence took a not-inconsiderable risk in cosigning with me. And I guarantee you I paid it back with interest. Once again, I'd been in the right place at the right time. I was able to take advantage of the chance.

Even after I got the loan, thanks to my friend Mr. Peaks, there was some legal delay to get through. The lawyer for Mrs. Atterbeary was a man named Lynwood F. Blount, who had a very successful civil practice. This same Lynwood F. Blount would be appointed to the Municipal Court of Philadelphia in 1973, one of the first black jurists to be accorded that honor. What I can say about this well-known man is that he gave me a hard time. I just could never get the agreement completed. I thought, *What is the matter with this guy? Let's get this thing moving here. I have this opportunity.* I remarked in a moment of angst, "Right across the hall from the office, there's a vacancy. I have half a mind to secure insurance and start a practice there and siphon off all the patients from your practice, and then you'd have nothing to sell."

I encouraged him, "Let's try to get this done. You seem to be fooling around and wasting time." Dr. Atterbeary's son came in, helped work out the deal, Blount finally agreed, and as of 1971, I had my own practice. Ida Atterbeary did not want to see the patients be lost, so by October 1970, I had already started seeing patients in the practice. My role was to keep the practice alive until such time as I could buy it.

The next few months were backbreaking, as I simultaneously got the practice started and tied the ribbon around my degree. Technically, for a little while, I was a postgraduate student who was also running a vigorous local orthodontist's office. Each challenge by itself incredibly involving. It was hard, time-consuming work. I started my workday at 7:00 a.m. and was seldom finished by 7:00 p.m., usually running late into the night with either patient calls or study. Looking at what I just wrote, I find it all hard to believe. I know I did it; I achieved the certificate from Einstein, the first black recipient in the program's history, and I purchased a practice that would be my livelihood for forty-five years. It was terribly difficult.

Hard work was something I was very familiar with, having had to work on the cotton farm for most of the first eighteen years of my life. The work I was doing at

Einstein and at my new practice was not physical labor, not literally backbreaking as my work had been in the 1940s and 1950s alongside my siblings and parents, but it was close human work. I had to be there. I had to care for my patients. I had to consult with them, listen, and look carefully, and I had to give them my best advice and best care.

I had to do many of the same things with my staff and patients alike. I was new and getting used to them, and they were getting used to me. I was determined to make it work. I took the subway all over town, or sometimes, I drove from my home, then in Mount Airy, back and forth to Center City to see patients or consult with my Einstein advisers. I took on these opportunities thankfully. I never looked upon any of it as "too hard" or "too much time," because I was used to hard work from my boyhood. I thank God every day that I had that opportunity and that it has worked out as well as it has.

I have enjoyed my relations with patients and staff. It has been a win-win situation for me. I can say that I have gotten as much from my patients as I have given. If you asked my staff, they'd tell you what my patients really think about me, and unless my staff is lying to keep the boss happy, what I hear is that my patients' feelings are 98 percent good.

I hope so. I hope I have been a giver, kind and considerate. For one thing, I need to do my best by the people who taught me, my parents, family, teachers, and classmates. I never forget what they taught me, the examples they gave, and the standards they expected. I bring them with me into the office every day, and I hope I have never let them down. For another thing, I had a business to grow, or as they may say today, a "brand to protect." I wanted to give good service so that satisfied patients would go away happy and tell others of their good treatment. I wanted to achieve a reputation of good care and of caring. People come when they need a helping hand. Medical care can't ever be all business. The human side is at once a business necessity and a moral imperative. My staff and patients got not only what the situation required but also what they craved, the human connection.

In June 1971, I received my certificate for completing my residency, and my life as a professional orthodontist had at last begun. My parents, sitting at home back in Greenwood, were thrilled. My brother David, who had always had a special eye out for me, let me know how proud he was of my perseverance and accomplishments.

## Growing a Practice and Building a House

I moved in to the former practice of Dr. Knowlton Atterbeary at that prime spot at Sixteenth and Walnut, treated his patients, and threw the door open to as many more as I could attract. I had a great office manager who managed well for many years and became a close friend. I was absolutely determined to offer my services to all colors and income groups. It was a diverse city; my practice would be diverse. I would see a lot of people who needed a lot of help with their teeth, and I wanted to give them that help. I opened my doors to all people when it came to hiring too. I had employees of all colors working in my office, not by design, but because they applied and had the best available skills.

I'm not minimizing dentistry when I say that I find my practice fun. I really enjoy coming in to work every day. Dentistry is, perhaps inevitably, an intimate line of work. You're working closely with people, working on their teeth. You're working on infections, extractions, prostheses, and braces. You do procedures that may provoke apprehension or discomfort, and you need a chairside manner that inspires confidence in your patients and allays their doubts and misgivings.

You also inevitably are asked for and must give advice. What's the best way to treat this misalignment? How long will it take, and what are the stages of treatment? What are braces, partial plates, retainers, bite blocks, headgear? I wish I have a dime for every dismayed look I've gotten from a girl or boy when I tell them they'll need braces and a different dismay on the faces of their parents, who see bills ahead. "How long will I have to wear these?" is one of the questions I've heard most, and there's much to explain: why braces, what we're looking to correct, when we have to tighten, loosen, or change.

Assurance is something patients crave, and I have to be very measured at giving it. And I'll often see signs that a patient may need a word or two on how to take better care of the teeth or appliance.

This means you get close to your patients. "You have to be good with people" is something you can say for many lines of work, from reporter to teacher to police officer. But in orthodontics, the practitioner and the patient often have a long-term relationship, as teeth and jaws take their sweet, natural time moving into better spacing and alignment, as bites equalize, as we get closer to the blessed relief, for me as well as for the patients and families, of the day we can take off the appliance and send a better smile into the world. It takes time and commitment, and there are questions at every turn.

I'd already gotten a taste for the human side of dentistry. I might have first caught the bug when hearing about dentistry from former coaches who had gone into training and become dentists themselves. It grew only stronger throughout my graduate and postgraduate training as I saw all kinds of patients, problems, and emergencies. Gentleness and human touch are all you need to gain the patient's trust.

Patients have told me for forty-five years that I have a good rapport with my patients. I don't just put braces on; I start hearing about your interests in school, piano lessons, triumph or defeat in soccer or baseball, dance recitals, talent for French or math or poetry. I hear about births, deaths, weddings, children, grandchildren. When I see you next time, I remember and I ask, because I want to know, "So how is X and Y going since I saw you last?"

Of course, I'm getting paid to examine and treat those teeth or that bite or that occlusion. I will bring my experience and training. That's what you've come for first and foremost. On that level, I have to focus on the problem. You don't want a dentist shedding tears when he or she should be paying strictest attention to problems and solutions. But beyond that, which is paramount in a professional sense, all my patients are individuals. I got to know families.

I was fortunate to come into a major city and capture a large proportion of the African American youngsters needing braces. I got the chance to sit and talk with them, care for them, and give them a chance to see a black professional who had done something for himself. Both children and parents alike told me this made their children felt good when they came into the practice for care. They were also encouraged that anything was possible in life. I felt proud to have a nice, well-equipped offices and worked hard to make this business prosper.

There was something else going on. Serving these children was a chance for me to ask them questions about their lives and to challenge them on certain things, their attitudes toward school, their hopes for what they themselves could achieve, their work ethic, and their dedication to their futures. I didn't blame them for being surprised at me or what I was. Most of them hadn't seen many black men or women in the professions or in any occupation of skill or authority. "You may be surprised to see a black man as an orthodontist here in Center City," I might say, "but not so long ago, I was your age, and back then, I couldn't imagine it either. But I'm here, so it must be possible." And if they asked, I could tell more of the story, the tough beginnings, hard work, false starts, misgivings, and the bedrock of a good family, loving parents, and high standards. What drew me to these young patients who called on me to take an interest was my own experience of people taking an interest in me. It's not so much that I was "giving back" consciously; it's just what I wanted to do for the boy, girl, or sometimes, family in front of me. I've probably had six or eight young patients over the last forty-five years who, after having a series of talks with me, later went to dental school. Not all were African American; two were white children who later told me they'd gone to dental school because of their relationship with me. When I first started, I saw African American students going into dentistry and related fields. It seemed to peak in the 1980s and 1990s and then to trail off somewhat in the 2000s. I wanted people to do what I was doing for the fulfillment of it, and for a way, it could strengthen communities.

That was when I got into telling stories, I guess. Patients and family members asked me to talk about where I came from, stories about growing up on the farm, many of which you've heard in this book. It's pleasant, of course, to tell stories about yourself, and it's said to be an old man's failing, so I tried to tie these stories into the patient's life or the issue we might be talking about, such as education, the importance of family, or hard work. Stories became a permanent part of my orthodontic practice.

Many patients grew to count on these talks and stories. I remember the patient who came into my office for a final appointment. It was that big day: after a long time with a retainer, she had come in to get the retainer taken off. I did so, performed the checkup, and with a smile, said, "Great! All finished."

But the little girl made a frown. "I not going to hear stories anymore?" she asked, close to tears.

My mother was a born peacemaker, a born negotiator, a person who could calm you down when you were angry, assure you when you had doubts, persuade you when you refused, change your mind when you thought you had it made up, and bring you together when you wanted to stay apart. Think of her taking us on walks over the land, listening to us, telling us things gently and unforgettably, looking right into our eyes. I should stress that this human and caring side extended beyond just us. She was always helping children, talking to them, and I could tell she often inspired them to try harder and aim higher. Being a farmer's wife, she didn't see many children day to day. Living pretty much on the farm, she tended to see only a fixed circle of people. But when she did see children, you could feel the spotlight descend on the child, a special soul in her eyes. She encouraged them in all kinds of directions. When they asked for help, whatever it was—cooking, housecleaning, going to school—she was there for them.

She could get along with anybody, and she raised children who were much the same in their lives. Think of my sister Mary Jean with children, my brother Clyde the teacher, my brother David the businessman. My dad contributed deeply to our human side too. He was the one who welcomed everyone to the table and drank and prayed with black and white alike. He was the one who urged me to recover from injury and excel, who wept when he put me on the bus to carry me away from the farm forever. But my mother was the one who taught us to work with people, see them for what they were, and be with them heart to heart in the world.

I have no idea whether I do this more or less than other orthodontists. From a financial perspective, you have to work with patients, schedule payments that they can meet, so they get their dental care and you get a livelihood. As with many health-care professions, you do a certain amount of work pro bono. People who cannot pay still need care and still deserve it, especially children without access or finances. I've worked with a lot of patients—worked very hard—to make sure it all comes out right. Most of them have upheld their end of the bargain. I won't say I have never been stiffed. For the most part, I'm glad to say people have shown that they appreciate the care and want to make sure they meet their payments.

I could tell many stories. I remember one gentleman brought in his twin sons. I looked into their mouths and saw two identical sets of the worst teeth I'd ever seen. The technical term *is massive anterior crowding and transposition*. It's just about as horrible as it sounds. Both boys had abnormal teeth that had come in terribly wrong. Cases like this are very complex and require advanced work. I learned in years of extra study that fixing these complex problems has to be done in steps and takes a long time. It takes patience, as the various braces and other measures coax the teeth into better alignments. I did some pretty hard work on those two boys, and I am glad and relieved to say it turned out really well. Toward the end of the process, I brought the father in and showed him the original casts of his boys' teeth from years before, when he first brought them in. He smiled in disbelief.

The satisfaction from such cases comes, of course, from seeing improvement in the teeth and in the lives of people. There's also a singular reward in watching the cooperation between what you do as an orthodontist and what nature does. Things happen on both ends. I can say that I was as proud of those twin boys in showing patience, long-suffering, and letting it all take its course.

Once, a white colleague of mine, also an orthodontist in the Medical Arts Building, came to me. "I have a patient I want to refer to you," he said. She was a little black girl who had a truly vicious malocclusion, an extreme misalignment of the upper and lower teeth when the jaws are closed. Her teeth were truly messed up, hard to look at. She knew it and was very shy. My white colleague apparently didn't want her in his office; he didn't like the idea of having her there, whether it was race or just the extremity of her condition. He obviously couldn't handle the striking contrast between this afflicted black girl and the rest of his patients. She was nine or ten, and each time she smiled, she covered her mouth because her teeth protruded so badly. I'm sure she suffered a great deal from bullying at school. I just had to bring her into care and make sure things worked out better for her.

Care is compassion, even when you get paid for it. Compassion is an art that must be learned. If I'm good at the human side of being a dentist, if I've been able to get children to see better possibilities in the world and in their lives, I credit my mother's example. I've said several times that in many circumstances, I was the first black man or the only black man, facing skepticism or hesitation. But at each level, stepping past self-consciousness, awkwardness, or resentments, I worked my way through and, in the process, made long-lasting friends and associates who'd later become very meaningful to me. I focused on my goals, knack for perseverance, willingness to work hard. At almost every turn, I was surrounded by people with better preparation, people expected to fulfill all standards. I won't tell you I never let all that get me down; I came close once or twice to turning on my heel and leaving. I didn't. I have all these beloved people to thank long past their own lives on this earth.

85

Now that I had my practice and was beginning to settle in, I had the collateral, with income coming in, and I could finally take seriously my longest-held dream. To tell the truth, I couldn't wait to build that house.

It was the early 1970s now, and my dad was past eighty. I could feel the reality of my dream closing fast. I had some financial leverage to get the project flowing, to pay the engineers, designers, and construction crews.

It was time to build that house for my parents. I couldn't stand the thought of them never having anything better than the same house in which they'd lived since 1919, the same house in which we all grew up. It was fine then; we never knew anything better, and I admit, sometimes I wasn't happy to let my friends see the hand-built house. Now, decades and decades later, it was time. David had spoken of having them live with him out in Portland, but I think that for Mother and Daddy, it was just too far from the rest of us, too far, too permanently far from her home in Mississippi.

For some time, I'd been having conversations with my brother Clyde back in Greenwood about it. You'll remember that Clyde was the homebody in our family, gravitating back to Greenwood, where he raised his own family, became a school principal, and held a variety of civic posts. He was in his midforties, in the prime, and well situated. So the plan arose that the house would be the home of both Clyde, his family, and my parents. The house would have two parts: one for Clyde, his wife (Rose), and their two daughters and an annex for Daddy and Mother. We could see a lot of cross-benefits. Daddy and Mother would always be close to family, and there might even be occasional babysitting benefits. Even as I managed my business, with plans to expand to other locations in the area, I was working with designers and construction firms to get the house started. As it turned out, the primary architect on the house had the surprising name of Johnny Mathis.

Believe me, it felt like a race to the finish. My daddy wasn't well, and I was hoping he'd get a chance to see the house I'd tried to dream into reality. As the crews down in Mississippi began the first dig, my daddy went into the hospital.

I had been keeping my plan a secret, so around the time the foundations for the house were being poured, I thought it might be good to tell my daddy. He was in his hospital bed when he heard about the house, and he said, "Oh, that child, he didn't need to go and do something like that."

Daddy died on August 1, 1974, at age eighty-four. He never saw those foundations or the house, but he knew it was being built, and he knew our mother would live there with Clyde and his family. I believe, and I've been told, that knowing those things made him grateful and pleased. I'm sorry he never had a chance to live there; I'm glad he at least knew that the house would be a reality. Daddy was a fair, humane, loving man who worked hard for everything he achieved. His family was the best fruit of his labors. I loved him deeply and think of him every day. My daddy will never leave me.

As the house neared completion, I sat down for a talk with Clyde and Rose and made clear to them that this was Mother's house. Rose realized what I meant. It wasn't that Mother had the right to invade her privacy, but the reverse was also true. Mother had absolute right to her own space. The house had been built in her honor. I wanted everyone to realize that the house really was hers.

When everyone moved in, Mother couldn't have been happier to keep the door to "the mother-in-law's annex" open for the kids. She loved her grandchildren dearly and let Regina and Dina come visit her just about whenever they wished. She wanted a free and easy flow between the two sides of the house. She was often with Clyde and his family, and they tried to respect her right to privacy, peace, and quiet when she wanted it. My mother would have ten good years in that house, and a very happy last decade it was, full of love and family. For all she had given for so long, we were able to give her that. And every day she got a chance to live with her son and daughter-in-law and grandchildren is a day for which I thank God.

## Growing a Business

As my practice grew and prospered, I saw we'd soon need to expand.

I had patients coming into Center City from outlying neighborhoods, such as Germantown and Mount Airy. I began to notice that some patients had begun to complain about parking and the commute for their children. It made sense to bring the practice to them, in a manner of speaking. So I got a real estate person to start site-shopping with me, and he found an office building on the corner of Mount Airy Avenue and Stenton Avenue in the Mount Airy neighborhood. It was a two-story building with two apartments upstairs and offices on the first floor.

Office decor and the whole atmosphere around medical offices were changing rapidly at that time, and I decided that for this new office, I'd order some really nice-looking decorations. This was probably one of the first such offices to have an open-bay treatment area. I wanted to make it a really nice place.

I threw an open house to introduce the new practice to the neighbors and prospective patients. It was a wonderful affair. A lot of my Einstein classmates came. My sister Colleen came all the way from California, which was very nice of her, especially since she almost died from the January cold weather. She said, "Next one of these you do, please have it in the summertime." But she also said, "Ben, I've been in a lot of dentists' offices in California, and this is the prettiest little office I've seen." We were very successful there.

Expanding a business is a complicated affair, very much hurry-up-and-wait, as you plan, design, line up money, location, equipment, staff, permits, legal and tax documents, and make sure the world knows about it. Expanding a business is a sign of good fortune; it means your business is healthy, flourishing, even bursting out to the extent that it's time to branch out to new places and set up businesses there. Above all, though, it's an act of hope. It means "I want to extend my services to an even larger part of the community. I want people to know we'll be in their neighborhoods, and I look forward to serving them." If I had not really valued the inarguable fact that my work helped people who needed the help—especially but not limited to the African American community, people who need the same dental care everyone else needs but often lack the means or outlets to get it—I would not have expanded.

## Losing a Mother, Gaining a Son

In March of 1983, after ten blessed and happy years living with my brother Clyde and his family in the house I finally got built, our mother died.

In her last years, we had a variety of chances to travel with our mother and show her a few things. She enjoyed herself. I drove from Philadelphia down to Greenwood and picked up my sister Mary Jean and our mother for a trip to Nashville, Tennessee. She was a big fan of country music, and so we took her to the Grand Ole Opry. We also traveled some 245 miles west to Knoxville and visited Knoxville College, the women's college she had left despite a warm and successful undergraduate career there to marry my father. I clearly remember her looking at class pictures, pictures of the class of 1919, a very small class of six women. I'd read the names, and Mother would tell me about each of her classmates, memory clear as anything, talking about what they were like, what they did together. We then brought her up to the Northeast. In New York, I took her to see *A Raisin in the Sun*, the play by Lorraine Hansberry. I also took her to Atlantic City, and of course, I showed her Philadelphia and my practice. I will never forget the time she sat behind my desk, and I told her, "This is where I call you from every morning." Most every morning, that's what I did. All she wanted was to hear my voice.

David brought her up to stay with him in Portland, Oregon. She stayed for about a month. The story is that she dressed up every day, and David took her to dinner. She visited Colleen and Mary Jean in California and stayed a few weeks there. By then, she was a little old lady, bun in the back of her head, skirt, stockings rolled up at the knee. She rose early every morning, as she always had. As much as she enjoyed her time with us, when she got back to her house with Clyde and his family, she soon went back to her old ways.

What an amazing eighty-four years she lived—born to a white father and his black housekeeper in a Jim Crow city; home-schooled when her New Orleans white cousins could take the bus to school; well-educated yet willing to drop her education for the love of a man who'd take her from her well-bred ways to life on a cotton farm for half a century of hard work; a tireless farmer, mother, adviser, negotiator, conscience, caretaker, nurturer, and role model; an absolutely marvelous cook; a woman proud of our daddy and of us; a woman whose greatest joy in life was her children and her greatest hope, our fortunes. Today, more than thirty years after her death, I take her with me everywhere. I work hard to deserve her, to uphold her great heart and good soul. But regretfully, my multiple unsuccessful marriages were something that she and I both looked upon as failures. Fortunately, she was always of a forgiving spirit, as I hope my former spouses are as well.

My father was already past fifty years old when I was born. I was forty-four when young Benji, my first and only child, came into my life in 1981. There had been something missing from my life, and when my wife gave birth to him, he made me forget all about it. I regarded him then, and I still regard him now, as a kind of miracle, a stroke of grace that went beyond understanding. Perhaps most parents feel this way about their children. I surely feel that way about Benji. He brought something into my life for which I am so grateful. He reminds me that, as much as our children owe us, parents owe them just as much the chance to have a life we'd never have known and to be people we never could have been without them.

He turned out to be Daddy's little man, and I took pride in being an active and attentive father. I changed his diapers. I got up with him, and we'd eat breakfast together every morning, and I'd make sure he was all squared away before I went off to work. On summer days, when he was three or four years old, I'd get home after a long day of work, and he was waiting there, and I'd get a hug and a kiss. If from time to time I would rather not spend time in the office, it was because I wanted to spend time with him.

There were a lot of days, I'll tell you, when my work left me pretty tired at the end of the day. It isn't so much that it's physically draining, but it is mentally draining. You have to regulate your staff, schedule appointments, and oversee the billing process. You have to work closely with people who often are in some degree of discomfort or anxiety. You have to field a lot of complaints about braces that hurt, about teeth that don't look good or don't fit together, about appliances that stick in the jaw or are uncomfortable. You're on all sorts of professional committees, you're possibly taking continuing education courses to keep up in your field, and you're meeting other people in the community. You're just kind of beaten up when you get home. I'd drive home just barely able to turn the wheel, get to our house, open the front door, and there was little Benji. And he'd say, "Daddy, I know exactly what we can do. Let's play baseball!"

Just what I needed.

I'd go upstairs, change clothes, get a bite to eat, and before you know it, I'd get a second wind, and we'd play baseball until the sun went down. He remembers those days with fondness now. We lived in the suburb of Gladwyne, with three-quarters of an acre around us. We had a nice backyard and front yard. That front yard was more level, and that was where we'd play. I'd bat him balls on the ground, and I'd throw him balls that were difficult to get and see how he could handle those. He loved that to death. After a day like that, I would be flat-out exhausted.

Later, I taught Benji how to play golf, which he enjoyed. Even there, he wanted to be like Daddy. I naturally first taught him to swing right-handed, but he said, "No, I want to play like you, Daddy." So to this day, although right-handed, he swings the golf club left-handed.

I love Benji more than anything. But it took him quite a while to find his way. That's both like me, as you now know, and unlike me. Like me, Benji attended several colleges. Unlike me, he never really found his way in education.

In recent years, Benji has told me, "I just didn't like school, I didn't like going there. I had fun with my friends, recess was a cool, but . . ." As a younger kid, he used to tell me, "I think they should have three months of school, then off for a month, then three months of school, then off for a month." His reasoning was that school schedules were based on an agriculture-centered economy, and we were long past that. And maybe he's right, or maybe he's the kind of kid who just wasn't cut out for school. His mother was an extremely good student, finishing high school at sixteen, finishing her bachelor's degree at the University of Massachusetts at nineteen. As you know, I ricocheted around until I landed at Kentucky State, going on a beeline from there, but all the way through, easy or hard, I really loved school, so I couldn't understand where Benji's dislike of school came from.

I did try a little to interest him in dentistry. When he was a little boy in middle school, I'd ask him, "Don't you want to be a dentist like your daddy?" His answer was "No, Daddy, you spend too much time at the office!" There might have been truth in that, and it might also have been that he and I got a kick out of each other and couldn't get enough time together.

My Benji certainly has brains and ability. When he was at school at the Episcopal Academy, then in Merion, Pennsylvania, his math teacher would ask him during tests to look away from his classmates, turn to the window, because he thought he was cheating. He'd read a problem, figure out the answer, and just write the answer down without showing his work. "Why should I show all my work when I know what the right answer is?" he'd say. "Why do I have to do all that? What's the point?" He can be very stubborn.

Naturally, his mother and I wanted him to go to college. My family was very competitive. We worked hard in school, and we were competitive about where we were going to college, what our majors were going to be, etc., but he didn't have any of that. He was a good student in school until maybe his middle school years. Around that time, my marriage to his mother had begun to suffer, and I don't know, perhaps that had some impact, but he didn't finish high school well. It was a bump in the road. He went to private schools all his life, and he saw many of his friends get into Ivy League schools, but he didn't have the grades. This didn't upset him nearly as much as it would have me.

His mother and I would try different schools and different plans, but it just wasn't for Benji. I did not try to push him in any direction, although I was always ready to help; I knew he had to find his own way. In later years, he has said he wished he did, after all, follow my footsteps. He looked up to my brother David and liked the idea of the businessman who works for himself, and that interest led him to get acceptance into the School of Business and Industry's five-year combined bachelor's and master's degree program for international business at Florida A&M University. Although he did not matriculate all the way through the five-year program (four years), he showed a talent for the business world and is currently doing sales and marketing for a health-care technology company in New Jersey. He now lives close to me, which is one of the great blessings of my life, and he hasn't said a word about going back to school. But he's a grown man now and can make his own decisions. Besides, I've just had to accept that there are some people school is just not for; that's another thing Benji has taught me. I applaud my son, Benji, and do the best I can for him. I pray for him every day. I am very proud of him. Like any parent, I feel joy and pride just looking at this person who has come into my world. I have enjoyed every day of my life with him and thank God for every day I've had with him.

## Business Is Business

I can tell you quite a few stories about my practice, not only what I did for my patients, but also what some of them did for me. I remember one Christmas, I was struggling for cash at that time, and I didn't know what I was going to buy little Ben for his Christmas presents. Well, word got around. I came home to find a Christmas card from the mother of a family I had treated. The father of the family was a veterinarian, and I had treated the children free, as one does, out of professional courtesy. But inside this Christmas card were five crisp $100 bills. I don't need to tell you how much such thoughtfulness meant.

Now, business was not all roses; it seldom is. It's true that my practices, whether in Center City or Mount Airy, have enjoyed success, and it's also true that they have brought me endless satisfaction. As my practice has grown and my roots have sunk deeper and deeper in the community, I have mastered ever more knowledge and skill in my chosen field. That itself was a source of great pride.

As I planned the expansion into Mount Airy, I thought it would be prudent to take a partner so I could lessen the burden on my own shoulders as the new practice grew. That was a disappointment; the new partner just did not pull his share of the load, and when that happens, you have to separate. And we did.

Occasionally, racial issues would crop up, much less so as time went by, but you ran into some uncomfortable moments. I'd run into them back at the dental program at the University of Kentucky. As part of our training at U of K, we would treat patients from the community. I remember one woman who came in, took one look at me, and said, "I want somebody else. I don't want him treating me." At that time, and any other time such a thing happened, the school stood firmly behind me. "We're sorry if you feel that way," my superiors would tell her, "but if that is your reason, you can't receive treatment here."

In the case I'm now speaking of, which happened once I had established my practice in Philadelphia, a colleague and friend of mine called me. He also ran an orthodontic clinic in Center City.

"Ben," he said, "I want to talk to you about something. I have a lot of secretaries and office workers and other patients"—his tone of voice told me he was trying to say they were white women—"and I'd like to refer to you all my young black male patients because these ladies don't want to sit in the same waiting room with them."

I said, "I can't do that. I refuse to do that."

"Well, I understand that. You and I, Ben, we know each other."

"Well, maybe you don't know me as well as you think," I said. Perhaps my friend did have a problem on his hands with women who had mentioned something or even complained. And he didn't want to alienate his employees or lose business. He could have funneled me thousands of dollars of work a month. But how could I have gone to sleep at night knowing what his reasons were, knowing that this is what we were doing? Those male patients had the same right to treatment as anyone sitting in that waiting room, and sending them to me because we were all black was basically a way to keep his white patients happy and resist integrating his practice. I was polite and professional, but I was firm in my refusal. To his credit, I suppose, he understood, and we remained friends.

Perhaps the most exciting incident was the case of the embezzler in my office. Even now, I can hardly believe I'm writing that, but I certainly had one. It was the mid-1980s, and she worked in my office and was one of my most trusted employees.

I had a big union contract, under which one of the local unions agreed to send me its members for their dental care. It was a lucrative contract, and I was to be paid according to a schedule of fees per patient and services rendered. But there are ways you can steal from a contract like that. Let's say you are the office worker I just mentioned. Let's say that one of your regular tasks is to keep track of the billing for my union contract. If you wanted to steal some money, you could charge the union for services and have them pay the money into an account. I hadn't done those services, and the account would belong to you, not to me. Those billings would be a lie, you could enrich yourself, steal from the union, and if you were sneaky enough about it, maybe you could get away with it. My office worker did just this for several years, under my nose, in my office, without me suspecting anything.

One day, who should show up at my office but the union rep I worked with, accompanied by a professional-looking woman. "We just want to see some of your files and go over some things," they told me. Assuming this was more or less a matter of routine, I said, "Fine, talk to the lady at the front desk and get the names you need." I had no idea anything untoward was going on, had no guilt, and didn't dream a trusted office worker had been stealing from the practice all this time.

I had no idea that the lady accompanying the union rep was from the Federal Bureau of Investigations or that I was being investigated for fraud by the union, for charging for fictitious services, which was a federal offense. It makes my hair stand up to think about it.

I first got wind of the legal action against me when a colleague called me up to say, "Listen, Ben, I have a patient who works at city hall, and he's just heard of a case accusing a dentist in the city of fraud. Ben, I think it's you. Your name has come up as a person dealing fraudulently with the union contract." I called my attorney that night, Nolan Atkinson Esq. It was a Sunday night, and we had an emergency meeting at the old Horn & Hardart Restaurant, and he laid out a plan and what I had to do, along with the costs.

The whole thing blew up in the worst possible way. I had trusted this employee and never thought she'd do a thing like that. And the case was brought against me rather than her. As a successful businessman and neighborhood figure, I was exposed. They took me to court, and I was suddenly fighting against an extremely ambitious young prosecutor looking to make a name for herself. She played hardball; she wanted the big name, which happened to be me. She wanted to get my name in the *Philadelphia Inquirer* or the *Philadelphia Daily News* and ruin my life.

I had to fight it. It cost me a lot of money and time. It also would cost me a great deal to recoup the business that was now gone forever, because the union withdrew the contract and stopped referring patients to me. Trust is everything in business, and once it's gone, it's pretty much gone forever, even if, like me, you're exonerated. Once waters are muddied, people rarely come back.

The case went on for what seemed like forever. A junior attorney in the law firm representing me told me comparatively early on that the federal lawyers knew they had nothing on me and that I was not guilty, but they kept looking and playing hard, all the way until the case was dropped. I had to sweat and suffer for nine months.

My employee was never prosecuted. They couldn't find anything against me, and they probably realized fairly early who the real culprit was, but they never went after her. As a big man, I was the person targeted, and when the case against me evaporated, the prosecutors lost interest.

I had read about such things in the paper, employees stealing from businesses and even from churches, but I never thought it would happen to me. I sometimes think that, if I'd had better insight into people and their lives, if I could have looked at my employee and realized something was going on with her, perhaps I could have cut this problem off before it germinated. Sometimes, too, I think that my very success, the fact that I was busy and on the go so much, relying on my office staff to keep things going smoothly, was part of the problem. Maybe I should have paid more attention.

As it turned out, my employee had some real problems in her life: a husband with medical issues and bills, a gambling problem, and lots of debts. I hated what happened, but I certainly never hated her. It did make me very sad. My slate was clean. That was what my parents taught me: honesty. Call me naive, but that lesson has stayed with me all my life.

None of these incidents in any way detracts from the rich rewards of working with my patients, talking to them, hearing about their lives, discussing things, especially with the kids. I've watched so many grow up, and I feel a certain degree of fatherly pride in them as they come into adulthood and find their ways. I also like seeing a good set of healthy teeth.

After opening my Mount Airy office, I enjoyed two decades of rewarding work before selling that business in 1993. I sold my business in Center City in 2010 after forty years of work there. In 2012, I began to offer services at several practices in New Jersey. I'm working for someone else, but in a lot of ways, it's like having all the fun and less of the responsibility. For most of my working life, I have worked five and sometimes six days a week. Now I go in two or three days a week, even as I'm nearing eighty, and I *still* sometimes find myself staying late. I guess I just can't stay away.

As a member of the community, I've been fortunate to meet a lot of interesting folks, people who help the world—or at least Philadelphia—go round. Through my beloved game of golf, I've made many sunshine friends, especially sports figures. I got to know Reggie Wilkes, NFL linebacker, while he was playing for the Philadelphia Eagles. I've been at golf tournaments at which I've met people such as Althea Gibson. In my early college years, 1956 to 1958, she had become the first black woman to win grand slam titles in tennis, winning the French Open, Wimbledon, and the US Open. She was also a very good golfer, playing pro golf for a while. And she was also a talented singer and musician. She was great to play a round of golf with, a sparkling personality, a very nice woman. I also got a chance to meet a very great golfer, Lee Elder, the first black man to play in the Masters and a successful pro golfer who worked hard for years to break the color line in a very segregated sport. It was intimidating to hit a tee shot with Lee Elder looking on, but he was unfailingly generous. A year or two later, I played two rounds of golf with Calvin Peete, another African American golfer who did very well on the PGA Tour. I also frequented the first black-owned and black-operated golf course in the country, Freeway Golf Course in Sicklerville, New Jersey.

One good friend I made through golf was Garry Maddox, who played center field for the Phillies for eleven of his fourteen Major League seasons. I met Garry when both of us were playing golf in a tournament supporting the Child Guidance Clinic that tested disturbed children. It was Garry who brought me in as a member of the Tough Luck Club. In the winter of 1980, right after the Phillies finally won their first World Series after ninety-seven years of trying, Mike Schmidt, the great Phillies Hall of Fame third baseman, and pitcher Larry Christensen started the Tough Luck Club, so named because several of the players did not have a great season previously; Tough Luck. Every January, we would go to Innisbrook Country Club in Florida and play golf during the day and party at night. And these were guys who could party. It was always a great time and a week I looked forward to, playing built-in tournaments during the day and eating wonderful dinners at night. The Tough Luck club included Schmitty, Christensen, Garry, longtime Phillies broadcasters the late Harry Kalas and Tim McCarver, pitchers Jim Kaat and Hall of Famers Steve Carlto,n and Ritchie Ashburn among other friends.

Through the Tough Luck Club, I got to be good friends with Richie Ashburn, the Hall of Fame outfielder, who played for twelve seasons for the Philadelphia Phillies, including on the 1950 "Whiz Kids" team that went to the World Series. He was an amazing ballplayer, with a lifetime average of .308. He led the National League in putouts from 1949 to 1958, and I read somewhere that of all baseball outfielders in the 1950s, he had the most hits and made the most outfield putouts and assists. Later, he broadcast Phillies games from 1971 until his death in 1997. Whitey, as he was called, was a great storyteller and joker, just a pleasure to have around. He was a smart man, quick on the uptake, who spoke his mind but also had a tender streak, which was why he made friends easily. Richie was a storyteller, and he gave me many insights into the way professional sports are run, including their racial policies. Richie told me, "Ben, you realize that even after Jackie Robinson broke the color barrier, all the team owners agreed on a quota of black players. It was that way for years. They'd had that 'gentlemen's agreement' for forever, in which all the teams got together and agreed they'd never hire black ballplayers. Once Branch Rickey broke that up with Jackie, they tried to hold the line, like Jim Crow baseball-style, and agree on a quote, 'this many and no more.' Same for football. Football held the line as long as they could." He also freely told me that he himself, as a young ballplayer, has not always reacted well to the advent of black men coming into baseball. "There's some things I did and said that were wrong, and I don't mind telling you," he told me, "that I'm very sorry about it."

We had a ball and never hurt anybody. I have great memories and great photos of all of us outdoors and indoors. Big smiles on all faces. When we roared into a restaurant after eighteen rather foggy holes of golf—and sometimes we really did roar—most places, no matter how full they were, would open up to us gladly.

## Giving Back

It has always meant a lot to me to remember those who helped me. From high school on, I kept my dream of building that house for my mother and my daddy for more than a decade, through college, dental school, an internship, and a residency. The moment I had the leverage to start building it, I got started.

The same holds true for the schools in which I learned my trade. As I've mentioned, I've pondered the decline in the number of African Americans who study dental sciences and start practices in the field. When I came up, and through the 1980s, you saw sizeable numbers of them. But those numbers dwindled somewhat into the 2000s, a decline that very much concerned me. For one thing, the black community always has lacked for sufficient medical and dental services, partly because there just aren't enough such practices where African Americans live, particularly in cities, and partly because, for better or worse, African Americans do not go into those fields in sufficient numbers, or if they do enter professional schools, their rate of persistence is much less than that of other students. Then there is the cost of such a course of study and competition from other fields that are now open and attracting African American graduates. As I told an interviewer for the University of Kentucky College of Dentistry *Perspectives* publication, "African American specialists in dentistry are hard to find, probably for the same reasons. It is unfortunate that I have found it difficult to find African American orthodontists to purchase any of the four practices I have had."

In 2010 I helped establish the Drs. Nero and Biggerstaff Diversity Scholarship Endowment at the University of Kentucky College of Dentistry. The other man named, Dr. Joseph Biggerstaff, was the first African American faculty member at the UK College of Dentistry, eventually being appointed to the chair of the Division of Orthodontics. Since the scholarship was established, I've devoted a lot of my energy to raising funds for it, and we've done pretty well in five years. It's for men and women alike, but not to get them into dental school; it's to help them once they're there. A number of students in professional schools are married. Often, they have homes, rent to pay, cars, and they can run into financial difficulties while in school. This scholarship is designed to help them when such trouble arises—to defray costs for books, instruments, and so forth. So we will identify eight to ten students in each year of dental school to receive scholarship money. We aren't limiting it strictly to students of color or disadvantaged background. As the university puts it, the scholarship is "awarded in accordance with UK's interest in diversity. Consideration is given, but not limited to, dental students who contribute to educational diversity."

In April 2014, my beloved schoolmate and friend Morgan Freeman came up to UK for "A Conversation with Morgan Freeman," in which he spoke of his life and his career. It was a conversation modeled on *Inside the Actors Studio*, the Bravo celebrity talk show. Playing the role of James Lipton was Barbara Bailey, an anchor at local TV station WKYT. At a reception afterward, Morgan mingled with people willing to give $1,000 or more to my scholarship fund. It was kind of Morgan to come down. He did, as he told me, because he knows how much it means to me. It was a real act of friendship. The College of Dentistry took some really beautiful photos of the two of us on stage and in various places on campus. I can't express how much that meant to me and how much it means that Morgan has kept in touch and retains a lively interest in how things are going with me, as I do in how he's doing.

I've met with students at the University of Kentucky, talking to groups of them about my experiences and my thoughts about the professions and the importance of diversity in those professions. Kentucky State, where I went to undergraduate school, heard what I'd done at UK and wanted to know whether I'd be interested in helping them out. I would really like to, but I am getting overwhelmed with such requests, and I have to respect my time now and get on to the things I enjoy doing in addition to working.

If you're the first African American to graduate from a particular professional school, as I was from the University of Kentucky and from Albert Einstein, people are pretty proud of that fact. I have allowed myself to feel pride in my work, pride when treatment goes well for patients, and pride when, as with the scholarship I just mentioned above, I can do something for other people who want to go into the same line of work.

Many were the times I started to take notes for a memoir then stopped or hired someone to start writing everything up, but the whole thing never seemed to get very far. During my frequent calls to and from my siblings, especially my brother David, we made plans to collect our memories and get someone to put them down on paper. He never saw that happen. One by one, my siblings joined my parents in death, Colleen in 1993, David in 2002, and Mary Jean and Clyde both in 2009. So now it's just me, which must mean it's time to get this thing written.

I return to memories of my walks on our land with my mother, side by side, sometimes hand in hand, question and reply, stories, jokes, staying close and getting closer. That scene of just the two of us fills me with nostalgia and love. It's almost as if we are the only two people on the earth, as if, for just a moment, the whole earth is ours, and we are free to roam where we want and say what we please to each other. Maybe, in this memory, the sun is setting, and it casts that brilliant, rich sunset light on her face, lighting her up, illuminating the two of us, and traversing those hard-worked acres. I know how much each acre meant.

Each acre represented the past we had come from, of slavery and Jim Crow, and of the hard labor of the generation born into one and having to live in the other. Those acres had been rescued from uselessness by my daddy's father and uncles, former slaves who bought the supposedly unusable land white men sold to black men for pennies, and then worked, as hard as they ever had as slaves, to clear it, draining the wetlands, clearing the woods, hacking out of an unpromising present a more promising future.

Each acre represented the work of a man of African and indigenous American ancestry, married to a woman of both white and black parentage, the work of having and raising a family, forty years' work. Those were the acres my mother and I walked, land on which my father and his brothers built that leaky old house in which we all slept, ate, studied, and grew up together. Those acres responded to my daddy's careful, knowing labor, yielding harvests year after year that kept us fed and in school clothes. Sometimes Daddy and Mother must have looked at their children, their hearts full, breaking, as they wondered what would happen to us. That was why they were after us always to do our best in school, to go to college, to get away, to have lives of our own. That, too, was what the land meant to us; it was what nurtured us, but it was also what we all had to leave. It was our origin but could not be our destiny.

My own heart is almost bursting as I realize that I can tell them this with the greatest, most blessed happiness: "All those years ago, when you looked at your children and worried about them, Mother and Daddy, you need not have fretted so much. We did all right. We turned out fine. We became public auditors, schoolteachers, orthodontists, businessmen. It was as you wished, even Clyde, who came back to Greenwood, came back a teacher and townsman. We had our own lives. You did well. You did wonderfully well."

I can tell them, "All of us carried your example and your teachings with us. We never forgot where we came from or who taught us, and we never forgot the point of working so hard, your work and later our work. You helped us see the point clearly once and for all. You gave us the timeless blessing of a meaningful life."

Wouldn't it have been wonderful if, by some miracle of foresight, I as a boy, walking with my mother over those fifty-one acres in Mississippi, could have turned to her and, to set her worried mind at ease, told her what would happen? If I could have seen the future, I could have said, "You know, Mother, your love saved us all, saved every one of us. We all went into the world knowing we were loved, and that led us forward. I'll leave the farm, last child of all, and you'll probably worry about me. In fact, Daddy's going to cry when I get on the bus going west. But you saved me too. I am going to do just fine. It won't be easy, and it won't always be smooth. I won't be perfect, and there will be bumps in the road. But I will always remember you, and that memory will make sure I do just fine. Rest easy."

No child ever gets to say that to his or her parents to set their minds at rest, knowing what life will be. We live in time: we have to to see how time turns out. But in the low sun of my memory, as I walk our land with my mother, I can look back over almost eighty years of my own on this earth and feel a great gratitude filling my heart. I realize that I couldn't have known then what my mother knows now. She rests easy in the love she gave us all.

# ACKNOWLEDGMENTS

I want to thank my son, Benjamin Jr., who has been more of a miracle in my life than I could ever have expected. He's encouraged me to write this book. I hope it helps him and his future family understand a little bit more about from whence they came. Thank you also to the patient faculty and staff at a variety of institutions through which I passed. All the people I just mentioned have my lifelong thanks. So does Morgan Freeman—he knows that, I dearly hope! So do other close friends, such as Charles Blackmon, Alexander Scott, Dr. & Mrs. John Moore, Alma Green (Henderson), Sallie Parfitt, all of whom, at different times, have been comforters, supporters, encouragers, and role models. I have a life of gratitude to offer Dr. Sheldon Rovin, my adviser at the University of Kentucky School of Dentistry, who treated me not only as a doctor but also as an equal, a friend, and a man in whom he took personal interest. He wasn't half-bad on the baseball diamond either. Dr. Stephen Dachi, chairman of the Department of Oral Medicine at the University of Kentucky, gave me extra work, some of the best advice I have ever gotten, and some very timely assistance in figuring out my next steps. I also owe a debt of thanks to Dr. Maxwell S. Fogel, head of the program in dentistry at Albert Einstein, for being skeptical about me and being extremely hard on me throughout my residency. I could see his pleasure when I graduated, tough though he was.

I owe thanks to Knowlton Atterbeary, who built up the first largely black orthodontics practice in the center of Philadelphia and who took an interest in a young black man working to graduate from Albert Einstein. And I hasten to remember with thanks his wife, Ida, who, when Dr. Atterbeary passed away, wanted me to take over his practice. Dr. Asad Sadiq, with whom I have been practicing for the last twenty-five years. Clarence Peakes, football player and businessman extraordinaire, deserves all my thanks for helping me purchase my first practice. So do many of the friends I've made in Philadelphia, including some Philadelphia Phillies, Eagles, and Sixers players, especially the late great Hall of

Famer Richie Ashburn, Garry Maddox, and Hall of Famer Julius "Dr. J" Erving, whose family was close and provided great times and memories for my son.

I want to thank my neighbor, the eminent journalist Claude Lewis, who sat with me for hours and listened to my nonsense, asking good questions so I could get my story out. Claude definitely did the hardest work on this book: he put up with me for hours on end, and he kept me focused on the necessary questions. Much in this book wouldn't have come to light without his patient work. He brought in fellow *Philadelphia Inquirer* writer John Timpane, who pounded a keyboard and made the material into something that is, I hope, readable. And of course, thanks to Donna Traz at Xlibris and the whole team there, who readied the manuscript for publication and truly made it into a book.

Now I must reach back. I want to thank my maternal grandmother, Leathie Davis, who managed to conceive and raise my mother from a powerless position. She survived being a black woman in a relationship, not of her own choosing, with her white boss. I will not name this man, although I think I know his name. I'd like to be somewhat more certain. But I can thank him for taking an interest in his mixed-race daughter, getting her piano lessons, having her home-schooled, and sending her to preparatory school and, eventually, to Knoxville College. I want to thank my paternal grandparents, the freed slaves John Tyler Nero and Henrietta Rennet Nero, for saving their money and making sure my father went to prep school and onward to complete his college degree. A huge thank-you should go out from all of us to the hundreds and thousands of people who sent money to endow the colleges, prep schools, and scholarship programs for African American students that arose in the last thirty years of the nineteenth century. They arose, and this great project of philanthropy arose, in an effort to offer education to a people so long denied it, in the hope that this would be a step toward changing the world. And it did—my family can testify to it. This generosity, so little remarked today, helped an entire generation. The first free black generation in our country's history realized at least some of its potential. Both blacks and whites contributed; they were an extension of the caring community.

In that vein, I'd like to thank the University of Kentucky College of Dentistry and everyone who has contributed to the Drs. Nero & Biggertsaff scholarship fund. It is an honor to pay it forward and help other young people realize their dreams through the dental profession.

My family, whose support and encouragement have been instrumental as I put the pieces of this story together. My nephews, Derek and Larry Nero and Earl Phelps. My nieces, Gayle Phelps, Regina Price, and Dina Givens. My cousins Geneva Patterson, Gwendolyn Loper, and others.

A special thank-you to the many members of my staff over the years, without whom I would not have been able to practice effectively for so long. Chief among them is my office manager and "adoptive daughter," Nancie Brown.

And now to thank people with no names—the millions who spent their entire lives as property, not people. I want to say to them, you have not been forgotten. Never believe I don't know that you too walk with me. I am but two generations removed from you; your industry, uprightness, and fellowship have shaped me. My parents were determined we would prosper, and they took that determination directly from you.

My final thanks are to anyone who reads this and takes something away from it. There is a message here. I hope that young people might read my story and connect with its good old ordinariness. Maybe they can see what they can achieve. I hope parents and teachers, anyone involved in family and school life, get a chance to read it. We are constantly debating the best means of giving children the greatest possible chance at a good life. Well, here's one example of many pulling together so children can succeed. Others have lived lives like mine. I don't want anyone to forget that. These are the stories that, as much as anything else, have shaped this country and can still teach us a great deal as we continue this experiment called the United States of America.

Dr. Nero's story resonates with me because it is a mirror of my Mother's story. Both from the segregated South "far from the farm" who had the audacity to come North for better opportunities for them and their families. Both fully recognizing that access to opportunity alone does not insure your success. A network of family, village, and community citizens who all read from the same sheet of music are also essential and required ingredients for desired success. The quality known as gumption ( my Mother's term) which I call moxie and which Dr. Nero embodies is required as well. Dr. Nero's story is one for our children to read and learn what dwelling in the realm of possibility looks like. This is a must read for parents of African American boys."

Hon. Blondell Reynolds Brown
Councilwoman At-Large
Mother of Brielle
Daughter of Sadie Reynolds

Through his vivid & cherished memories of growing up on a farm in Greenwood, Mississippi , Dr. Ben Nero has added immeasurably to the understanding of African American life in small town USA in the late 1940's & 50's. More importantly, he has poignantly depicted his childhood against a backdrop of violent racism, but also amidst a nurturing black community in the Jim Crow south....his parents, siblings neighbors and teachers, a few of of them white, and all of them intent on seeing him & other black children achieve far beyond the exiguous successes, hard wrought from the scraps left to Negro families just two generations post slavery. In his new memoir, "That's The Way It Was", Dr. Nero eloquently reminds us all as American citizens, that our foundation was established by individuals like him, and families like the Neros of Greenwood.

Lisa Thomas-Laury
Former ABC News Anchor
Philadelphia, PA.

My husband, Charles Blackmon would be extremely proud of this book. Charles and Ben were classmates and good friends during their formative years and remained close friends up until Charles' death in 2005. Through the years, Charles shared many of their Greenwood, Mississippi stories and experiences with our children and me. Reading certain chapters in the book brought back fond memories and joyful moments for which I am truly grateful..

Ben has done an excellent job of telling his story.The book is a must read not only because it provides a glimpse into a large African-American family's life in Mississippi but also highlights the successes of Black children who grew up in a time and place when educational opportunities were not equal. Although the schools may have lacked adequate space, equipment, books and supplies, the students excelled anyway because of teachers who were smart and talented as well as resourceful, dedicated.and nurturing.

Thank you Ben for sharing your story!

Betty Reynolds Blackmon
Widow of Charles Blackmon

# INDEX

My paternal grandparents John Tyler and Henrietta Kennett Nero

A portrait of my lovely mother, 1980

This wonderful man is my daddy, David March Nero, in the early 1940's when he would have been in his 50s.

The house in which I lived after 20 years of being unattended, 1990s

The house I built my parents, next to the old house, 1974

David Nero
1924-2002

Clyde Nero
1929-2009

Colleen Ruth Nero Phelps
1929-1993

Mary Jean Nero
(1932-2009)

All of us. (1956)

Dad, Clyde, Jean and me

Thomas Williamson (WR),
Herman Lawrence (RB), and me (QB).

High School Prom

Back Row Standing: Rufus Russell, Susan Gunter, Lonnie Love, Albert Peacock,
Gabriella Taylor, Charles Blackmon, Grace Dillard, Alice Gilmore, Benjamin
Nero, Selwyne Rias, Ethel Markham, Alexander Scott, Annie Henderson,
Claudette Anderson, Mary Jean Smith, Barbara Curry, Doris Syfax, Jo Ann
Hammons, Thelma Scott, Curlee Mcafee, Griselda Jordan, and Alma Green.

The end of a wonderful era.

Graduating class from UK College of Dentistry.

The result of four years dedication.

113

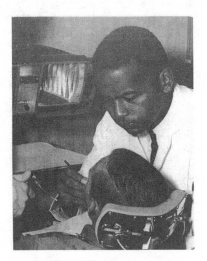

My first job out of college as a Histopathology Technician w/ my colleagues, May B. Cason and Wendy Martin

My first patient during year as a dentist, "Scared to death."

A picture of me in an operatory for a profile for the Philadelphia Inquirer.

The legendary Althea Gibson, Wimbledon Champion and LPGA Tour member and I at Freeway Golf Club.

Mr. Lee Elder, first African-American man to play in the Masters and I at a tournament in Richmond, VA.

Pretending to be a big leaguer. "Phillies Dream week in Florida."

115

Three friends and
I playing golf at
Springfield Country
Club. (left to right,
Larry Benning,
"Buddy" Chester,
Morgan Freeman,
Myself)

One of my many trips
back to Kentucky to see
my friends Becky and
John.

Dr. and Mrs. John Moore

Two friends reunite for a
wonderful cause.

UK diverse scholarship
fund.

Daddy's little man.

Mom and baby Benji.

Daddy watching the Eagles
while Benji naps.

Visiting Uncle David in
Portland, Oregon

With my brothers David and Clyde at
Benji's Christening in 1982

Coaching Benji's Baseball team.

Me, Benji, Mike Good, and Morgan Freeman

After a round of Golf at Merion Country Club Home of the 2013 US Open.

A young lady whose education I sponsored in Haiti.

Mom in college in 1917.          Mom and Dad's 50th Anniversary.

This photo was taken around the 1900s near Greenwood,
Mississippi. – The Willis Nero family